WHAT PEOPLE ARE SAYING ABOUT

FINDING A WAY

Finding a Way Ahead! is a valuable b
shares her personal thoughts and ex   pplying the
perennial truth of the Bible to the concrete circumstances of life
in the 21st century.

She shares her reflections on the words of hope and guidance
found in scripture in an accessible and readable way.

The message that prayer, coupled with positive words and
actions, can be used to overcome challenges is a relevant and
timely one.

This book would make a useful pastoral aid and provide
stimulation for prayer groups.
Sheila Donohoe, B.A. (Hons), PGCE and CCRS

With prayer suggestions, points to ponder and practical suggestions this book is useful for both small group and individual
reflection.

If you ever ask yourself how to spiritually handle different life
situations, then this book will certainly offer valuable food for
thought
Annette Hayes, B.A. (Hons), PGCE, CCRS

How often do we tell people 'we're alright', when asked 'How are
you?' Many of us don't want to reveal our worry, fear, our shame
or just the pressure and uncertain future that we face. *Finding a
Way Ahead!* is the book that can really help you.

The author shares her own experiences, and especially an
amazing testimony of healing, together with a number of Bible
stories and 'prayerful conversations' both with the Lord and with
friends to help us move from panic to peace, from fear to faith,
from hopelessness to happiness, from grief to the godly use of

gifts. She invites Jesus in to help solve the confusion and uncertainty that we are facing.

We are all walking the same road of life, we are wanting to see the 'way ahead' clearly, but sometimes there is darkness, doubt and even death. The author provides us with some positive and encouraging signposts and God-given promises that will give us confidence for the future.

Finding a Way Ahead! is a book to read from cover to cover, but it is also the book to leave around so you can turn to one relevant chapter in a time of need. It is also the book to pass on to others as a gift with your love and prayers.

Canon Michael Cole, Editor of Living Light Bible Reflections, Nationwide Christian Trust

Finding a Way Ahead! is an uplifting and unique guide to healing. Ideal for anyone living with a chronic illness who is hoping to find new strength from within. The author Angela uses her own experiences of living with a serious disease and how she found strength in learning to love herself more and appreciating all the positive things in life.

Una Rose, author

I am happy to endorse *Finding a Way Ahead!* I found that it contained many pearls of wisdom to help people see the brighter side and to help with problems. It is very difficult for many of us to "forgive those who trespass against us", but this book certainly provides some valuable pointers.

Ray Pallett, author

I have known Angela and her family for many years. In her book, she explores, with great empathy, the many issues around hurt, fear, suffering and the more painful challenges of life. The whole book is a letter to the reader, engaging us in a conversation drawn from her experiences and others, of suffering and recovery of health.

Most importantly, not only does Angela emphasise the possibility and need of learning from our painful experiences, but she also reminds us again and again that the blame (against ourselves, others, or God) that so often attaches itself to suffering is a burden we need to deal with and remove on the way to wholeness.

Angela offers devotional help and coping strategies for us to begin to think beyond our anxiety and hurt, and even to begin to plan for the future God offers us. This is a book to reflect on and keep dipping into.

Revd Bill Eugster, Baptist Minister, Glendale Crossing Places, Wooler

We all experience difficult times in our lives and these are, for better or for worse, very formative. They can strengthen us or destroy us. Christianity, with the cross at its centre, has much to say about dark times and the hope of finding the light. Angela Harper has written an essentially practical book to help people in these difficult times. She bases much of what she writes in the personal experiences of herself and others. The practical nature of the book makes it important for those who want to know what to do rather than discuss why it is happening! I found her words on self-worth and dealing with low self-esteem especially helpful.

Revd Robin Eastoe, Team Rector of Heavitree with St. Mary Steps, Diocese of Exeter

Angela has a desire to see all set free by Jesus and to know life to the full in Him. Reflecting on her own painful experiences of herself and others, she shares what helps her to release the past and to grow in becoming all God wants her to be.

Revd Steven Hembery MA.FCA., Senior Minister, Leigh Road Baptist Church

Finding a Way Ahead!

Spiritual signposts to healing
and wholeness

Finding a Way Ahead!

Spiritual signposts to healing
and wholeness

Angela Harper

With a foreword by Canon Michael Cole

Winchester, UK
Washington, USA

First published by Circle Books, 2016
Circle Books is an imprint of John Hunt Publishing Ltd., Laurel House, Station Approach,
Alresford, Hants, SO24 9JH, UK
office1@jhpbooks.net
www.johnhuntpublishing.com
www.circle-books.com

For distributor details and how to order please visit the 'Ordering' section on our website.

Text copyright: Angela Harper 2015

ISBN: 978 1 78535 418 2
978 1 78535 419 9 (ebook)
Library of Congress Control Number: 2016937657

A CIP catalogue record for this book is available from the British Library.

All Scripture quotations in this publication are from THE MESSAGE.
Copyright © by Eugene H. Peterson 1993, 1994, 1995, 1996, 2000, 2001, 2002.
Used by permission of NavPress. All rights reserved. Represented by Tyndale House
Publishers, Inc.

Design: Stuart Davies

Printed in the USA by Edwards Brothers Malloy

We operate a distinctive and ethical publishing philosophy in all
areas of our business, from our global network of authors to
production and worldwide distribution.

CONTENTS

To my family and friends – thanks for listening to me, and helping out!

Preface

Finding a Way Ahead!

Welcome to my book. So many of us have times when life suddenly changes from the one we've known, to a life that's quickly become scary, and insecure. We can be so bewildered and shaken up that we find that, we've lost our way ahead through illness, disability, loss of self, bereavement, and disempowerment. There are so many situations where any sort of security we may have once had has vanished. How do we navigate our way through unknown realms? When we go through suffering it is helpful to look at our responses to this, in order to understand what is going on in the depths of our souls. Throughout this book I have indicated useful coping mechanisms for people going through a range of different life experiences to help them find their way back to safety. The techniques in this book can also help those who are searching to connect with the intelligence of our universe in creative and healing ways, so they can find God in a way they may have never experienced before.

The book looks at healing, but emphasises that although we may earnestly and desperately pray for the healing we want, we may not get exactly what we have asked for! God always has the final word! It seems to me that we all have vocations which often thread their way throughout our lives, shaping us for a particular direction, and where we can use our knowledge of any particular suffering we have encountered in order to help others. I do not believe God sends suffering, but sometimes our experiences equip us in extraordinary ways to grow into the people we were meant to be, and identify with those who need someone non-judgemental to talk to. In this way everything we have been through God recycles, uses, takes away, and heals in some form, (even if we are unaware of how God is working in the background).

I believe it is often during our most difficult times, that God starts to open the windows of our souls in order to let the light flood in and reach what is inflicting us. Sometimes we may find that all that has distressed us starts to fall away or we feel unexpectedly lighter. As the windows open, everything suddenly gets an airing, and starts to surface as God brings it out to heal. (This can be quite painful, but sometimes the pain barrier needs to be gone through in order to reach empowerment.)

As you go through this book, I pray that the windows of your soul start to open, and that you start to feel better. It is not your fault in any way, if you have not received the healing you want. It is too easy to blame ourselves and believe that we haven't been heard because of a lack of faith! Any prayer, however it is formed, contains faith which cannot be measured. It is not in our power that miracles happen, but that of a vast Trinity who is infinite, and far beyond all the imaginations of our minds!

Three years ago I was dramatically healed from a life-long lung condition, fulfilling a prophecy I had received some ten years before that. I had attended a retreat where one of the people who worked there, told me she had been shown a picture in her mind, telling her that I would be healed. After hearing that, I prepared for my healing everyday – knowing that God had asked me to co-operate while the healing was taking place. During that time my health actually became much worse, but I looked at and improved all of those aspects of myself which were looking for wholeness. I am sure all of this self-analysis contributed to the great healing I was to encounter.

Although some of these writings are from a personal perspective, the content also reflects the experiences and struggles of others, especially those who may be feeling margin-alised and finding it hard to adapt to society. The latter have yearned for their voices to be heard, which is why I have included them. Other writings are inspirational and written in the first person so a reader may be able to identify with them. In this way, I hope that a wider readership can identify with the situations or feelings described and use them in a positive way. All of this contributes to our gaining a wider perspective when we are struggling through the hard times – a common theme for all of us. I do hope that you find these thoughts beneficial and that you find some wisdom which can help you to heal.

In my case I had to wait until the illness had served its purpose in order for God to remove it. On the particular day that I was healed I was feeling quite ill when unexpectedly, I was aware of a huge shape being removed from me by an angel who had suddenly appeared. My illness had been taken from me and then my health recovered. We all struggle with life in many different ways, and this can mean that we lose our way, and find that the outcome of our healing and the direction we so desire is out of our control. All we can do is to co-operate with God's help to find our way back to the path we've lost, or to find a new way ahead.

My book is split into small sections – ideal for busy lives, and it can be carried and read on your way to work, or while you are waiting in a queue! I do believe I was guided to write these thoughts, and I pray for you to be refreshed and uplifted as you read through each section.

Finally, I would emphasise that this work is not intended to be a theological discourse, or overly religious, or academic, but rather it seeks to help people find the spiritual keys to healing and wholeness in a creative way. Jesus working alongside self-help!

Angela Harper

Acknowledgements

My thanks to all those who have offered me advice and support: Michael Cole, Una Rose, Ray Pallett, Robin Eastoe, Bill Eugster and Steven Hembery (especially for Steven's attention to detail in reading the early draft).

Also to Tim for giving me permission to include his idea of what L.O.V.E can stand for:

Lots Of Vital Encouragement. I'm sure my readers will find this beneficial.

Foreword by Canon Michael Cole

How often do we tell people 'we're alright', when asked 'How are you?' Many of us don't want to reveal our worry, fear, our shame or just the pressure and uncertain future that we face. 'Finding a way ahead' is the book that can really help you.

The author shares her own experiences, and especially an amazing testimony of healing, together with a number of Bible stories and 'prayerful conversations' both with the Lord and with friends to help us move from panic to peace, from fear to faith, from hopelessness to happiness, from grief to the godly use of gifts. She invites Jesus in to help solve the confusion and uncertainty that we are facing.

We are all walking the same road of life, we are wanting to see the 'way ahead' clearly, but sometimes there is darkness, doubt and even death. The author provides us with some positive and encouraging signposts and God-given promises that will give us confidence for the future.

'Finding a way ahead' is a book to read from cover to cover, but it is also the book to leave around so you can turn to one relevant chapter in a time of need. It is also the book to pass on to others as a gift with your love and prayers.

Michael Cole
Editor of Living Light Bible Reflections produced by The Nationwide Christian Trust

About Canon Michael Cole

Michael has a long experience of ministry in Leeds, Sheffield, Manchester and Woodford Green, Essex. He was involved with the South American Mission Society for many years and is currently editor of Living Light Bible Reflections and a contributor to Living Word on Premier Radio.

Personal note from the author

When I approached Michael to see if he would endorse my book, I was delighted that he offered to write a Foreword for me; I was so pleased! He has a wealth of knowledge and experience as a minister, a writer and broadcaster, an editor, a listener and supporter of people who are finding life hard whilst managing a health condition, or encountering hard life experiences.

Angela Harper

Chapter One

Caring For You

Things to Think about – Loving Yourself

'Love others as well as you love yourself.'
(The Message)
Mark 12: 31

Looking at yourself – once you love yourself, life and health tend to improve because you are no longer beating yourself up

It's not easy for some people to love themselves. Some believe that it's narcissistic or selfish – but to love yourself means that you are more able to achieve the realistic things you want to do in life, without constantly thinking that you are not good enough; loving yourself means that you are able to comfort yourself. Loving self helps to look at the world through that framework, which helps to take situations or people in a more realistic way rather than by using a wrong interpretation! It also provides a secure foundation that can better enable you to help others.

Self-love is a protecting factor which enables us to build a safe haven deep inside. However, so many of us speak negatively to ourselves, which often means that we can often hold grudges against the things we, ourselves, have done, even in our childhood! It's always best to look within and see if we have done anything causative or unjust. After that it's good to learn from it, to understand why we did something wrong, and then repent, and start afresh with our slate wiped clean. To accept forgiveness for ourselves is not easy in a person who doesn't love who they are, because they can hold onto un-forgiveness instead of being able to release themselves. In that case learning compassion for who you are can help this process. If you have never felt loved, start by appreciating you, because you must have been strong to have coped so far.

A short story about you!

You can only be you, because that was who you were created to be! You can never be anyone else, even though you may have yearned to swop yourself for someone who in your estimation is far more worthy! Everyone around us will always have different gifts and unique faces, but that is them. Do not deny yourself by wishing you away, use your gifts – we all have them. It is so easy to lose self-worth. From childhood onwards we all hear criticisms, and somehow they take root deep inside us. Some of these criticisms are lies told to you by people who judge others rather unkindly, and can never see the beauty of another person. Often these people have never felt loved, so there is a reason behind their harshness, because this is how they feel about themselves. Deep down they may even feel desperate, and this comes out in their sharp criticisms towards others.

Do not believe you are worthless, or ugly. Everyone is beautiful in a different way, and we cannot compare looks, or our individuality, because we all have a purpose for our souls. All our lives are tailored in a personal way, life is often painful, but you have learned so much that is of great value. Don't put down who you are, these are just reactions to the pain you're feeling. Ask God to turnaround you, so that you can now be unhindered by the circumstances which may have trapped you into a small cage. Now it's time to soar, and let yourself out.

There may be aspects of learning that you find hard to handle, or something may have happened which has stopped you doing the career you so longed to do. But you have two treasures – yourself and God. When you pray you will not be denied your dreams, although you may have to wait for them. If they are not beneficial for you, something else will open up which will be more suited to you, and this will prove to be far, far better in the longer term, (even though for now you may not believe this).

We can all learn from others of every age, from children to those who have reached one hundred, and beyond! Everybody has a sprinkling of wisdom in some way, do not limit yourself to just your peer group, do not look down on those who are 'different' everyone has something to teach us. Choose your friends with great care, and look after them, but don't let them use you. When we nurture others, we also nurture ourselves, men are just as good as nurturing as women!

It's time to value you, at the moment you may feel poor in spirit, so appreciate the small things that happen every day, such as birdsong, fluffy clouds in the sky, and the rain which glistens like diamonds when the sun comes out to shine, after a stormy time. Sometimes others seem so much more capable than us, but don't lose your life in wishing to be them. We can all do something well, and we can learn to polish up our gifts, but we must get them out to use, we can't keep concealing our beauty, our ways, and the gifts we have.

We are all of equal worth, and our minds and thoughts function uniquely, no one can be you, as we can't be them. You are you for a purpose; the most important thing in your life is to get to know you! When we start to love ourselves, life flows more easily, and new opportunities are more likely to come our way, because we now feel able to take them, and grow.

If you keep giving your feelings of disempowerment to God, watch how they start to fall away like a landslide, and see how new events start to happen, in the way that God plans. Learn to stop any unhelpful reactions, and turn away from the habits you've struggled with – when you see someone you believe is far more worthy than you – how do you know? You are judging yourself rather harshly, as you may have been judged before by others. This does not mean you have to continue seeing yourself through other people's darkened images of you. Welcome you today! Celebrate the good you may have done, and any achievements, whatever they may be!

Live! Talk kindly to yourself, and vital new starts can happen! It is never too late to do this!

What did that passage say to you?

Notice how you felt while reading that passage. Did you refuse to receive it, or did you believe it? If you once again rejected yourself, try talking to yourself kindly as a nurturing parent can talk to a child and then work on reframing certain thoughts about yourself. So many of us seem to stick to the same script when we think of us! So it's just re-writing how we may learn to love ourselves without repressing or denying anything. By talking to yourself kindly I believe that is how the Holy Spirit talks to us. It may feel strange or odd at first, but over time, self-love, plus more tolerance towards others can build up.

Are you feeling trapped and living by approval from others, when all you want to do is to be the real you, and fulfil your vocation but are scared in case others do not accept you or what you believe you are called to do?

Often when people find that courage to let go and be themselves they become more genuine and alive, and this can generally help in feeling better.

A friend of our family believes that each letter in the word L.O.V.E. means Lots of Vital Encouragement because we all need this at times to use both for ourselves and others.

We've all been hurt by other people and/or experiences – we need to take time to understand what keeps triggering our inner wounds, even when the event is past. Are you still reacting, and basing your whole life on the same wound? It's taking time to give the whole experience to God and ask for help.

Unconditional love can be found in this life, when we start the search; God makes sure that we find this divine love. Imagine God's light and love shining on you today, notice any helpful thoughts; are all your friends good ones? Are there any people or circumstances hindering your progress? Are you allowing people to put you down? Do you put yourself down, in front of other people? Take some time out to read this passage from 1 John 3: 18-20. Try and read it every day, and let it reach those places in your soul which need help.

What does real love feel like?

My dear children, let's not just talk about love; let's practice real love. This is the only way we'll know we're living truly, living in God's reality. It's also the way to shut down debilitating self-criticism, even when there is something to it. For God is greater than our worried hearts and knows more about us than we do ourselves.

(The Message)

1 John 3: 18-20

Conquering Fear!

As soon as the meal was finished, Jesus insisted that the disciples get in the boat and go on ahead across to Bethsaida while he dismissed the congregation. After sending them off, he climbed a mountain to pray.

Late at night, the boat was far out at sea; Jesus was still by himself on land. He could see his men struggling with the oars, the wind having come up against them. At about four o'clock in the morning, Jesus came toward them, walking on the sea. He intended to go right by them. But when they saw him walking on the sea, they thought it was a ghost and screamed, scared out of their wits.

Jesus was quick to comfort them: "Courage! It's me. Don't be afraid." As soon as he climbed into the boat, the wind died down. They were stunned, shaking their heads,

**wondering what was going on. They didn't understand what
he had done at the supper. None of this had yet penetrated
their hearts.**

(The Message)

Mark 6: 45-52

Fear!

I'm sure most of us have been kept awake at night because of fear,
even after praying for the healing of it. Some fears loom so large
it's as though they threaten our very being, and as we look up at
those fears, it feels as though they are devouring us. Our prayer
relationship with Our Creator and our prayers to make things
right for us are anything but easy, because we can't see God
physically. As a consequence we all imagine God differently and
it's hard to concentrate on how we think Jesus may look or
respond while we pray. Indeed when a fearful situation remains,
we desperately wonder how we will get out of it. From the
suffering of fear our whole self can feel at constant threat. Some
fears are so huge (whether imagined or real) and our response
can be so troubling, giving rise to sleepless nights, terrors, palpi-
tations, sweats of horror, that we believe our very response could
destroy us.

Our imagination is a gift, we use it to pray, to create, to think.
It can also help us form our very personalities, and discover who
we are by showing us our gifts and likes and dislikes.
Imagination is a great power, but there's also a downside, and
that is when it takes over and starts to over-process fearful situations. When we face these things our minds can go round and
round locked in that cycle of fear that remains before us. When
that locked cycle happens, our minds are actually trying to help
us process it, and as the fear circulates continually, the mind is
doing its job by trying to solve it, and unpack it. Plus our mind is
trying to alert us to a thought pattern that could be unhelpful.
(Strangely, this is the mind's way of working for us, by using

repetitive thinking, it can finally rest when the fear has been looked at, understood, and a solution found or fear let go.)

We understandably fear when our very survival is at stake, if we believe we are going to be attacked, or we are seriously ill, etc. Indeed there are many fears and a myriad of causes, which often go back to some traumatic event earlier in our lives that we have not really recovered from. However our fears manifest themselves, whether they are real or imagined, they are often still homing in on a particular event we once went through. Because that fear keeps coming back, it can be telling us to look at it deeper, to see what it is really telling us. Life is far from easy, and there will be fears that we have to face, with no running away. Of course, other fears suddenly happen with no past experience to look at.

Perhaps we could imagine that we are slowly ascending white flights of stairs which are bringing us closer and closer to God, but as we go, and grow, new challenges suddenly appear. This is a parallel process because as we walk up the stairs Jesus accompanies us to either remove the obstacle of fear, or to lead us through it safely. What may have once distressed us can suddenly give way to more helpful reactions; this is when we overcome and find that we may have experienced a spiritual promotion.

The passage of the terrified disciples on the stormy sea comes just after the feeding of the five thousand, where the perplexed disciples wonder how they can feed everybody, which is when Jesus tests their own powers of faith wanting them to have enough faith to manifest the food. After this event when Jesus had demonstrated another lesson of His power to feed the five thousand, a new challenge comes upon the disciples when they are caught up in a storm. It must have been violently shaking their boat from side to side. I'm sure when Jesus looked down from the hill where he was praying to see the distress of the disciples he thought "What? They still don't get me, (the all-powerful God) and my promise to look after my creation!"

It might be helpful for you to imagine that you are in the boat alone with the storm raging, and any minute now it will threaten to capsize you. At this moment the fear is horrific because you don't feel able to swim, and you really believe that you are going to drown. Indeed you might be fighting for your life in this instance. All of a sudden you see a figure walk towards you on the water, and as it is night you wonder if it's a ghost. (In Jesus' time people were generally frightened of the sea because of the unknown things that might live there.) It is then you realise the figure is Jesus and it looks like he will pass you by, but instead he climbs into the boat with you. At first the storm carries on raging, then the waves appear less agitated, next they start to calm down and settle, and finally the water clears for you to see the sea bed clearly. Of course during this time, Jesus is holding onto you. The fear is now calmed and the cause of it might be clearly seen and understood, as Jesus starts to work on it with you. (Sometimes the healing of fear does not immediately take place, if the fear remains there is something to learn about it before God removes it. Whatever happens, The Creator will show you when the time is right for it to go. Praying for the Healing of Memories can also be helpful.) Eventually though, you will be able to look down on that fear having finally overcome it, rather than look up to it which makes a fear dominant.

There is no blame for the fear, whatever it is, and you may have to wait for insights and divine help to be provided in order for you to resolve the fear you now clearly see. God may teach you to let go of the fear, or show you how to face it. (Jesus will be alongside as He walks through the fear with you.) Whatever happens you know God is on the case, as a light shining on the particular fear. This can help restore a calm-ness, despite circum-stances still prevailing, and the power and confidence you have gained in God (and in yourself) while being in the boat with Jesus helps you once again to trust, that somehow all will be well.

There can be a feeling of moving through the fear, as you once again walk up the white stairs, in a process of growing closer and closer to the unconditional love of God.

Whatever the fear, God will not refuse to help you grow and to bear new shoots, we're not alone as the Holy Spirit comforts and teaches us. It is a triune activity; God, Jesus and Holy Spirit, the divine three, interact to make us stronger people, you will never be judged for being fearful. Fear is one of our inbuilt survival skills. It aims to protect us as it sounds alarm bells within us so that we can escape from harmful situations. It's only when it moves in and takes a hold of us that we need help. Even if we are still perplexed and wonder how we will get through, we have the promise that God will be with us and rescue us.

We Are More than Conquerors

So, what do you think? With God on our side like this, how can we lose? If God didn't hesitate to put everything on the line for us, embracing our condition and exposing himself to the worst by sending his own Son, is there anything else he wouldn't gladly and freely do for us? And who would dare tangle with God by messing with one of God's chosen? Who would dare even to point a finger? The One who died for us – who was raised to life for us! – is in the presence of God at this very moment sticking up for us. Do you think anyone is going to be able to drive a wedge between us and Christ's love for us? There is no way! Not trouble, not hard times, not hatred, not hunger, not homelessness, not bulling threats, not backstabbing, not even the worst sins listed in Scripture:

They kill us in cold blood because they hate you.
We're sitting ducks; they pick us off one by one.

None of this fazes us because Jesus loves us. I'm

absolutely convinced that nothing – nothing living or dead, angelic or demonic, today or tomorrow, high or low, thinkable or unthinkable – absolutely *nothing* can get between us and God's love because of the way that Jesus our Master has embraced us.

(The Message)

Romans 8: 31-39

What this passage says to us

These verses were written by Paul at a time when persecution and great suffering was about to be inflicted upon the believers. Paul's assurance to us now, as then, is that when great trials happen to us, we are not abandoned or separated from God, even though we all go through those journeys. (These trials are allowed to happen for many reasons; either we get to know God and ourselves deeper in those times, or we grow in a new direction which is our vocation.) Paul also addresses the times when we know we've sinned – (gone against what we know to be the loving essence of our true natures), so that we can really know we're forgiven, and can receive that forgiveness. Paul also assures us that, even though others may wrongly judge us, and we are aware of their wrong viewpoint, we are not judged like this by Jesus, who sees into everyone's souls, and understands our behaviours, and the way we are. This is the true sacrifice of Jesus, which can be hard to take in, when we compare His unconditional love to the harsh realities of the world around us. Our lives in every way are redeemed, even though we may still struggle through many things at times. How often we can be put off, not believing the love God has for us, because other's judgements of us, have taken a hold, and we wonder if Jesus thinks the same! He doesn't!

As we pray about how others may have judged us, you can ask for the gift of good indignation! In this way judgements can be overcome. Others will always do what they want, but you are now, not kept prisoner by these situations. You will find that they don't bother you so much, and this can allow divine love to enter. Now you know that it really doesn't matter what others think, it's only what God thinks, which is far more positive!

Affirmations – we are more than conquerors!

Affirmations are popular in our current culture; they're in nearly every book about self-improvement. What Paul seeks to tell us is that we are more than conquerors. If we quote scripture as affirmations from the Bible, they can have a positive and transformational effect. When we keep saying 'I am more than a conqueror' before we face a difficult situation, we may not believe it, because it has no life at first. Then after saying 'I am more than a conqueror,' a few times, it may start to resonate and give the power to turn what seems to be an unsolvable situation to one of resolution.

Years ago, I knew I had to face a very difficult person in my life, so actually I invited him round! As the hours ticked on to our meeting, dread came over me! Then it was as though the Holy Spirit reminded me 'I am more than a conqueror,' and by using it as an affirmation, and thinking about it, the more it became real!

When he turned up, there was a noticeable difference. It was not a particularly easy meeting at all, but the whole situation had been turned round to one where it was now malleable. Situations are not always instantly sorted out by Jesus, often, for a while, we are left with something we don't like hanging over our heads. However, these things can be left for a purpose, because ultimately God can see a blessing in it for us! How we turn situations around is just trusting in this divine power to do this. Behind the scenes of the everyday ordinary life, the divine works ceaselessly for us.

Through affirmation, scripture has a way of becoming alive and real, it talks to our souls, and it cuts through the incessant chatter of our minds. It can also be useful to quote scripture when we are ill, because the body may start to respond, and you may start feeling better, because everything has a consciousness in some form. Affirmations in the Bible can come alive when we quote them, and these can help us to gain the victories we need!

You may need to find a variety of affirmations to use for different situations – and these are contained in God's promises which help them come alive. For instance, my favourite passage in the Bible is Matthew 6: 25-34. Whenever I am stressed I am always directed to this passage. This helps me to realise how we can take off and let go, as though we are flying, because we can only do so much, while God does the rest, we are here to live; The Trinity is here to rescue us. If we worry then we can remain grounded and cannot take off and fly!

I'm sure you will find passages from the Bible which speak to you, and if you keep repeating them in your mind, they gradually come alive, restore, heal and rescue. Here are some of the verses from Matthew 6 which help me.

"If you decide for God, living a life of God-worship, it follows that you don't fuss about what's on the table at mealtimes or whether the clothes in your closet are in fashion. There is far more to your life than the food you put in your stomach, more to your outer appearance than the clothes you hang on your body. Look at the birds, free and unfettered, not tied down to a job description, careless in the care of God. And you count far more to him than birds."
(The Message)
Matthew 6: 25-26

Chapter Two

Our Inner Wounds

I'm Wounded God, and it's Affected My Relationship with You – Do You Care?

Show me that you care, why have you allowed so much to hurt me in my life?

"Don't bargain with God. Be direct. Ask for what you need. This isn't a cat-and-mouse, hide-and-seek game we're in. If your child asks for bread, do you trick him with sawdust? If he asks for fish, do you scare him with a live snake on his plate? As bad as you are, you wouldn't think of such a thing. You're at least decent to your own children. So don't you think the God who conceived you in love will be even better?"

(The Message)
Matthew 7: 7-11

It is a common experience of those who have been hurt by others to wonder if God will hurt them too! Is this where you are?

Someone's prayer about 'un-met' needs...

Dear God
I'm still waiting for all my prayers to be answered God, and I've had a long wait! Some of the requests I've prayed for throughout my life and still, they're unresolved, and I feel left with them, as though you don't care! All of this creates a lack of trust in me, as though you take pleasure in playing hide and seek with me, one minute you're there, the next you've gone. Then I wonder if you're out to trick me, as so much of my life has taken me when I'm unaware and off guard, as though you've

been sneaking up on me ready to catch me out, and wanting to prove that I'm so sinful, there is no hope for me! Surely there's other ways of kinder testing than this! Do you have to be so cruel? Are you a good, God?

AMEN!!!!

The divine reply!

My child,

I've heard your prayers so many times! The desperation, the hardship, your inability to let go. It is as though you believe that refusing to let go or not letting me in is protecting you from getting hurt again. You cannot bare your soul to me, because you believe that I too, may hurt you like others have. But this is not so! My love is not conditional and, although you may experience pain and worry, I always hear your prayers and act! Sometimes in the middle of this I make sure that we connect while you are looking at the beauty of a clear sky, a sparkling sea, an orange and red dawn or the white purity of snow in a crisp winter. But then, suddenly your vision of me changes like bad weather brewing, and now it becomes stormy and grey! I know of everything that has worried and disturbed you. It is all here in front of me, and, for your benefit, I ask that you reach out and trust me to help you with all the burdens you have, which, as yet, have not been answered in the ways you have wanted.

I see your life from an aerial perspective, and so much I allow in your unpredictable world is to produce bravery and compassion. I would never play hide-and-seek, or tricks on any of my children. There are so many misconceptions of me in your world, but my thoughts are far **above** your earthly plane. Some of the burdens you have carried, which you feel are unbearable, have helped you grow in other ways. It is for your growth I have allowed these things. I haven't been careless with your needs, and I haven't been ignoring them. Why would I create an infinite universe, and create lots of children, only to leave them to it? This doesn't make sense to me, I have a personal relationship with each one of them, even if they do not know me, I still created them.

I often work in ways which are quiet and undetectable. So often my children may not have sensed my working, but now recognise that something has changed. My promises are real, and it's time for a new start, you can trust me, even when my plans for your life oppose those you have made for yourself. My renewal with you will be blessing you with new reactions to situations, and opening your eyes to see me clearly and to understand my workings. When this happens we will share a unity, so that you will know you can trust me. You can give me everything which worries and hinders you, and I will help you to have a life of great benefit, more than you could ever believe. What was once impossible for you becomes possible when you really want to get much closer to me. I won't let you down, I answer your prayers in my ways, watch how your trust grows. I am the indulgent, warm, loving parent! Not the one that's out to get you!

I am your loving Creator – your God.

Feeling Weary

"Are you tired? Worn out? Burned out on religion? Come to me. Get away with me and you'll recover your life. I'll show you how to take a real rest. Walk with me and work with me – watch how I do it. Learn the unforced rhythms of grace. I won't lay anything heavy or ill-fitting on you. Keep company with me and you'll learn to live freely and lightly."
(The Message)
Matthew 11: 28-30

Help! I'm feeling trapped!

Are you feeling tired, or fed up with the same things going on in your life? Maybe everyday seems the same? Are you feeling trapped in a familiar cycle, where nothing positive seems to be happening?

Firstly, try and give the things that are bringing you down

over in prayer. Then try and get on with your day, appreciating the good moments which will happen now and again, as Jesus is always stepping in and out of our lives. Sometimes we put an intense effort into insisting that God makes things better, and there are days when it seems as though we don't get anywhere. So what's the point in praying, when we're trying to do everything we can? The point is that, whether we have handed things over to God, or not, Our Creator will always answer us in ways that meet our needs.

Something that Jesus did was to get away and be alone in prayer for a while, and we too can do this. It takes us away from our own circumstances, even if it is only for a short time. Maybe you could pretend to be a tourist and visit your own locality; there might even be a local landmark where you've never been? Well today's the day! Every area has something worth seeing, and being proud of. We may be living where we are for some divine purpose, so why not get acquainted with where you live? You may find that whilst exploring your area in quietness and prayer it is made clear to you that you are going through a time of healing and preparation, and you need to give yourself time for this to take place. You may also discover that a number of questions suddenly appear in your mind, and this is often when God asks us to take a fresh look at the life we've been living.

You may find a multitude of questions (which are relevant to your situation) being posed, which need much thought and God's help to answer. These questions from God will be different for each of us, but some of them may be:

"Are you too scared to use those gifts you've got in the ways I've asked you? What is the fear that you feel you cannot face about using your gifts? Can you find My presence? As I am always with you to help, can you accept my offer of help to re-create you, and bring out your gifts? They, like you, are of great value."

"Are you so busy in life that it is hindering your search for me? If so, are you using work to bury your issues instead of letting Me help you heal them?"

"If the way ahead is not clear, please surrender to Me rather than strive and force your own plans. I will work with you, and see that your needs are met. Do you trust me enough to realise that I am responsible for you?"

"Why are you serving yourself? I haven't called you to serve Me in the ways you've been doing!"

"What are the ways I've called you to help Me to help others?"

"Helping Me is about being my friend and taking time to talk things out, and appreciating our friendship. Sometimes I just ask people to be and not to get caught up in an outward busyness. Ways of prayer, quietness and contemplation are very much needed. This can often clash with how your friends live their lives when they seem to need a job title or status to feel worthy. How will you cope with the reactions they may have towards you, when they believe that 'you are doing nothing'? This is, of course, not true because you have a different pattern for your life, and I will provide for you. Ask Me for any help to heal this now, so that you will remain true to Me, rather than listen to the world's reactions."

Taking time out might mean that you are posed these questions, but don't worry if you don't hear anything from God, for we can't force it. God's presence is in the stillness, and the company that God offers. If you cannot find the divine companionship, then ask for your perspective to be altered, so that you can find it.

You may also stumble upon a vital future purpose whilst walking in your locality while you pray, think and reflect. This could be something you've never even considered before! While you are busy praying, can you find a place to eat, is there somewhere new to indulge in any local food produce? Time out is also about treating yourself, so that you can be built up once again. Don't forget Jesus came so that we could have life in abundance, if money is tight, can you visit your favourite place, is there a view you long to see?

The Unjust Judge – A Journey through Low Times

Jesus told them a story showing that it was necessary for them to pray consistently and never quit. He said, "There was once a judge in some city who never gave God a thought and cared nothing for people. A widow in that city kept after him: 'My rights are being violated. Protect me!'

"He never gave her the time of day. But after this went on and on he said to himself, 'I care nothing what God thinks, even less what people think. But because this widow won't quit badgering me, I'd better do something and see that she gets justice – otherwise I'm going to end up beaten black and blue by her pounding.'"

Then the Master said, "Do you hear what that judge, corrupt as he is, is saying? So what makes you think God won't step in and work justice for his chosen people, who continue to cry out for help? Won't he stick up for them? I assure you, he will. He will not drag his feet. But how much of that kind of persistent faith will the Son of Man find on the earth when he returns?"

(The Message)

Luke 18:1-8

Something goes wrong... our faith gets low; we arrive at the conclusion that God is an unjust judge!

Are you feeling as though you're stuck and your prayers aren't

24

getting answered, even though you are constantly praying for the same thing to be healed and resolved? Maybe the situation you are involved in, whatever it is, is wearing you down, and day and night you plead with God to sort this out for you. Sometimes you might even imagine that you are desperately banging on God's door with your fists, as though God's the unjust judge in this parable!

We might get angry and shout through clenched teeth!

"I've been patient with you for a while, but my patience is running out, how dare you allow this situation God! It's wearing me down." (You shout at what you perceive to be the closed door of God.)

"I've had enough of you God!"

"Please, please sort this situation out for me God, NOW! I CAN'T WAIT ANY LONGER! WHY ARE YOU TAKING SO LONG?"

And so it goes on and on, and indeed you might just feel as though you're involved in a battle with the Almighty, as you start telling God what to do, and imagining that your requests aren't even heard!

Eventually after continual pleading and praying you might just become more than a tad worn out! Darkness has come over you, as the light of faith within you disappears to no more than a tiny flicker. Depression or sadness can easily engulf you in this state, and you might suddenly come to the conclusion that there's no hope for you! It is though, quite safe to get cross with God and shout! We do have a faithful friend who understands our situations, and sometimes it's just waiting for God's timing. I've discovered that when our needs are being sorted out they're ordered in a series of stepping stones, first this, then that, and so on. It's as though we can't have our needs fulfilled by the second stepping stone, until the issues on our first stepping stone have been sorted out by prayer. There's a divine organised order amongst the chaos of our lives. Imagine our lives in a heavenly filing cabinet, where all the moments of our lives and all the things we've suffered, are filed in an immaculate order. Sometimes it's as though God says "Not yet, you need to have patience and wait, while I sort out and heal the first things that need to be removed/resolved/healed." Often we don't even want to hear that, because we need it NOW! Then in our waiting we can forget, or don't believe that God has promised to help us.

It's easy during this time of waiting when we need something so very badly to perceive a warped picture of God, and believe that we have an Unjust Judge in control of the whole universe, who wants us to wait for ages and ages, so there! Our spirits can sink to a state where we come to believe that we have been denied an answer to our prayers because we have become restless in our long time of waiting. So we continue through life feeling dejected and alone, forgetting that our prayers are always answered in God's way, not ours! After all of this, we can find ourselves, suddenly feeling guilty of mistrust, and needing our hope and faith restored, but we really don't know how to do this. It's as though our faith can't even get off the ground and yet we want it to fly into the air like an aircraft; flying confidently to the right destination. During this time, we carry on serving God in quiet desperation, because we don't know what else to do, or we need to keep on doing things just to keep occupied! It is this carrying on and serving, come what may, which gets rewarded despite our faith running on a low flame. Helping God by serving in the ways we've each been led to blesses us through what we have given.

(When we think about serving we don't just mean serving in a church, you may be continuing to act in many other ways that are considerate and helpful to others, despite how low you might be feeling.) Then, as if out of nowhere, you achieve a breakthrough and something like the following happens:

"I see what you've done. Now see what *I've* done. I've opened a door before you that no one can slam shut. You don't have much strength, I know that; you used what you had to keep my Word. You didn't deny me when times were rough."
(The Message)
Revelation: 3 8

In the midst of it all, we can find ourselves given an unexpected verse about a wonderfully open door, and we find to our horror and joy, that the door to heaven has always been open to our prayers! It's so easy to have put any childhood experiences onto God – some of us, when we were children, might have seen our parents as omnipotent, and we can sometimes project their failings onto the Almighty! Maybe we have also been sucked down by the circumstances surrounding, us or others, which have stopped us seeing God as loving, sovereign and in control!

"Oh no, what have I done, I've lived in doubt? Sorry!"

Helping to restore our faith then, might come through a sermon, repetitive messages from God that appear in our minds, or a friend ringing us while feeling prompted to tell us something. Help always comes, we are never left hopeless, and we discover that we have been enlarged in the waiting. Next, it's so important to ask for our faith and attitude to be corrected, so we can help the process of restoring ourselves and helping to ease, manage and overcome the situations or health issues we might find that we are in. After this time of blackness we can give to God the hopelessness which we have just felt. We then find that we need to ask for our low faith to be transformed into a life-enhancing existence of a trusting child-like, faith. So we discover that, for our prayer request to be brought about, we might also need to do our own bit of co-operation, whilst allowing God to do the rest.

We can affirm our thanks as we ask for a child-like faith, which always trusts and expects, whatever the outcome which is chosen for us. Trying to keep our new resolve of a child-like faith will also help us feel so much better as we are not using all our energy to continually beg in our prayers. Once again we can live in hope, and while we do this, we find that God won't fail us, as divine promises made, just for us, are always kept, while we keep trusting too.

Our Gifts Can Be Forged in the Hardest and Darkest of Places

"I'll lead you to buried treasures,
secret caches of valuables –
Confirmations that it is, in fact, I, GOD,
the God of Israel, who calls you by your name."
(The Message)
Isaiah 45:3

Darkness

Valuable gifts are forged in times of darkness. Often our lives consist of seasons where it is so dark we really are scared and don't know the way ahead. Many of us go through long-term illness, bereavement, loss of security, abandonment, and times of bewilderment where we feel totally lost, we feel loneliness and doubt of self, and a sense of captivity. However this feeling of captivity may stem from the experiences God is tailoring to prepare us to undertake a specific mission. There could well be a cost to ourselves, as we wonder if we will be able to cope with it all, but these circumstances are a necessary training for the task ahead. All of the above can cause us to feel trapped as though we are contained in a tiny box, where we rummage around frantically for the light to find us. Sometimes what we desperately want healed, is not healed, and we then find we could not have done the mission God wanted us to do, without it.

During these times of darkness and wanting to confide in someone, we may well find that others don't understand where we are coming from, and somehow this backfires on us, and once again we feel left with what's going on in our lives. We can often feel isolated in a way where we cannot find any comfort, and we wonder if we are the only ones who have ever felt this way?

These times break us while they forge us into new people; often we've found we've had to cope while we feel so burdened and this is where we are taken beyond where we can go, and so, we are expanded as people. To get through the hard times we've had to use the genetic gifts which we may have inherited, our own natural gifts, plus we've had to create our own gifts in order to help us get through every day. All these will merge with the gold and purity of the specific gifts which God has given us to create something incredible. Sometimes all these boil down to us creating our own survival strategies in a valuable, priceless, handbook which we have written in our minds in order for us to cope.

Amazing gifts and new growth then have been created in misery, and often, when we feel we can't go on any further in the dark season we find ourselves in, God comes to our rescue. This happens in many little ways, so keep a journal to record these rays of light. You will know when things are getting better, because you may start to feel more released bit by bit, as you suddenly find God cared all along, and cried alongside us! The Trinity is at work for us as three divine, distinct personalities merge together: Jesus the divine saviour and healer who comes alongside us, God the indulgent Father or Mother, or Creator, (however we see God), and the Holy Spirit who walks with us and daily gives us life, breath and instructive, helpful, inner chats. All this somehow comes together when they know we need it, and at the same time, we can find ourselves being repaired, with a newness, and a new personality, and where we find that

God is actually friendly after all! Suddenly we can be shown a new direction and a new healing, where we may actually feel cared for by the Trinity, and where Jesus can start to feel so real and not remote. This is often where we are given an understanding of all that we have been through, so that it all makes sense.

We can use the gifts that were forged in the darkness to help others, and as we do so, we can nurture and heal ourselves at the same time

Can we identify our gifts?

Even when we have not identified our gifts, we often use them without realising it. We may believe we are waiting to use them, but often we're constantly in service without knowing.

Here are some gifts you may have created in order to survive, these are priceless treasures, your trophies; these are highly prized by an indulgent and loving God, who we may discover is proud of us and how we have coped.

Gifts

Openness, where your vulnerabilities are a strength. (Use these skilfully where you don't invite distress to yourself by telling all, use this gift for those who need it.)

Being alongside someone, listening, and just being there.

Wisdom and life skills – can you help and teach anyone who has gone through a similar life experience to you?

Nursing (this doesn't mean you necessarily have to have a medical training) this is a gift for caring and mopping up after someone! (A very specialised gift!)

Creativity (art, music, writing, creative problem solving, loving new challenges), this is one where people who have these gifts just have to keep creating. Is there anyone you can help to inspire with these gifts?

Crosswords (do you have the patience and logic to teach those who might want to do these as a new hobby)?

Maths and finance, very valuable; are you able to help a person budget and get their life back in control financially?

If you made a handbook of Survival Strategies in your mind in order to get yourself through a really hard time, can you help teach these gifts to others who are going through similar experiences?

Hospitality, and helping people get on and talk – (making people welcome with a friendly smile, is everything, as this helps to dissolve other people's defence mechanisms and barriers which they have needed, and probably still do to protect themselves).

Cooking – are you an incredible cook especially where you have had to budget on hardly any money, and yet create wonderful dinners? Can you teach others these skills?

Do you have attention to detail – can you help people fill in forms? This can be life-saving.

Can you teach other people new thoughts to help them break the vicious cycle they may be in?

Often people can feel as though everything is against them, so can you help show them any rays of light in their lives, and another way of looking at things in a more uplifting way?

Are you contemplative or meditative, can you help anyone find a stillness and a safe place within them? This is a gift which is everything, so many people seek it, and yet so few find it.

Generosity – do you have time to give others? So many people feel that no one is interested in them, and no one wants to hear their story, can you hear them, and help them rewrite their story in their minds as an epic novel? We all have epic lives, none of us are ordinary, none of us can be labelled, can you help others celebrate their individuality and diversity, and yet integrate with them?

Map reading, and teaching how to make sense of bus and train timetables! A very necessary skill that others may not have learnt.

Secret dreams in your heart, what are these, how can you use them? These are gifts which are wonderful when someone uses them, because they can aid a huge growth.

Are you a brilliant gardener and can give people beautiful gardens where they can relax in?

If you have a career – can you help others train and find employment?

Teaching – does anyone need some extra help if they missed out on education?

Drama or theatre skills – helping those who need more confidence in themselves to fulfil their potential on stage or in life?

Driving – this is such a skill, being a safe driver, and passengers actually wanting to be in your car is a compliment! Is there anyone you can give a lift to who cannot drive, or has mobility issues?

Encouragement – helping others find their gifts and use them.

Have you just uncovered a new amazing gift that you have not recognised before? If so, what is it?

A prayer of intimacy and thanksgiving in finding a new relationship with God

A seeker's prayer

Dear Jesus,

It's me! But then you know it is! I've been struggling so long to find the real you, I've looked here, and over there, and in every corner of my inner being! I've even been from church to church, and gone to House Groups. I've asked different people of varying faiths how they see and know God, all to help me find the real you. Everyone has taught me some wisdom and I've sifted out those bits from others and myself which I didn't agree with, because all of us have some beliefs about you which are a tad tainted. For a while I even thought I had to earn my way to get your attention and approval, and help, so I kept myself busy serving you everywhere, and I overdid it, because I became ill! I've also analysed myself so much, and found that I've done things I'm ashamed of, and I sometimes wonder if I'm a good person. As you can see, I've been a bit frantic, and I've got tired trying to prove myself to you!

Today, as I was carrying on as usual with all of this, I believe you spoke to me, butting in on all those busy thoughts! It was so clear, that it cut right through my thought patterns, so I knew it was you. Actually you seemed so nice and friendly, I know now that you share all my pain, because you know it already. Before I was born you knew what would lie before me, all my mistakes and all the things I would excel at. You've been with me, even when I've been unaware of this! Yet you still believed in me! You've taken on everything I wasn't able to do, you've redeemed those times where I've been ashamed, and you've been faithful in helping me bear some heavy burdens.

While I'm talking to you I'm also thinking about those deep sorrows which remained with me every year. I really didn't know how to handle them, so I asked some people to help me with them, only one understood, while the rest gave me some strange looks, as my losses were outside of their experiences. Today though, a clear picture from you emerged in my mind, and you thanked me for going through all those unbearable circumstances because they helped shape my being and my vocation. You then promised that you will put an end to them, and you held out a box for me to put those traumas in, which you then assured me you will seal and put away deep within you, where those memories cannot harm me again. I will then, keep putting all that has distressed me in your box, until I feel emptied and relieved of them. Those memories may remain so I can learn from them, but you will no longer allow their sting to hurt me.

Thank you so much for turning up! I do at times think you're rather slow in coming to my rescue, but you were there all along, quietly observing, protecting and guiding me! I'm feeling lighter as I think about this! I now know that I don't need to continue being so frantic in trying to find you, your spirit lives in my life all the time, but you acknowledged my search and came through for me. You are aware of my thoughts at all times, and you send blessings into every day which I know I've been careless in observing, and therefore I haven't thanked you for them.

Everything we go through has a time and purpose with you, until it has reached the end of what it was supposed to do, and then you remove it. You are like a gardener, willing me to grow and blossom, and when that flower has died, you then replace it with a new shoot that will burst into bloom once again. It has been so wonderful to have found you in a new, real way, I always wondered what it would feel like, but now I know! I've been praying to you throughout my life, but I never knew your comfort and reassurance until now. All I can say is that I feel different as though you and I have now suddenly merged, I live in you, *and you live in me. There is a new completeness in me, I have come home. You let me search for you to test how serious I was in finding the real you, and now I know you are so much nicer than I expected! You are preparing me for a new start! How can I fear with you beside me? Even though I know I will at times get busy and lose the consciousness of your presence, all I have to do now is to relax and connect! Thanks!*

Amen

Chapter Three

Burdens We Carry!

Zacchaeus

Then Jesus entered and walked through Jericho. There was a man there, his name Zacchaeus, the head tax man and quite rich. He wanted desperately to see Jesus, but the crowd was in his way – he was a short man and couldn't see over the crowd. So he ran on ahead and climbed up in a sycamore tree so he could see Jesus when he came by.

When Jesus got to the tree, he looked up and said, "Zacchaeus, hurry down. Today is my day to be a guest in your home." Zacchaeus scrambled out of the tree, hardly believing his good luck, delighted to take Jesus home with him. Everyone who saw the incident was indignant and grumped, "What business does he have getting cozy with this crook?"

Zacchaeus just stood there, a little stunned. He stammered apologetically, "Master, I give away half my income to the poor – and if I'm caught cheating, I pay four times the damages."

Jesus said, "Today is salvation day in this home! Here he is: Zacchaeus, son of Abraham! For the Son of Man came to find and restore the lost."

(The Message)
Luke 19: 1-10

Zacchaeus was a tax collector, overcharging and keeping some money back for himself. The passage demonstrates that Jesus actually wanted to connect with and redeem this dishonest person (like we've all been in our own ways), over dinner. You can imagine, Zacchaeus was really enjoying his extravagant lifestyle supported by charging people too much tax, but, it's also possible that Zacchaeus hated himself for the greedy habit he was indulging. Zacchaeus probably felt desperately alone with the habit coupled with a deep guilt and a sick feeling of shame. If Zacchaeus was feeling like this, then that would have made him all the more keen to find freedom from this and meet Jesus.

This must have been why he climbed a tree to see him, so Jesus couldn't fail to see him! When Jesus saw him and approached him as a friend, instead of berating him, Zacchaeus probably felt the relief that Jesus already knew where he had gone wrong, but at the same time Zacchaeus now knew that after all he had done, he was still loved. Maybe you could imagine the relief which flooded Zacchaeus, this must have helped him give his overcharging habit to Jesus so that Zacchaeus could receive the power to make amends and repay anyone whom he had overcharged.

Jesus saved Zacchaeus from himself, and in that time of Zacchaeus giving Jesus his burden, it was as though a swop was completed – Zacchaeus gave Jesus his habit, and in return Zacchaeus was given power and insight as to how to correct his wrongdoing. One of my friends always says Jesus recycles our situations when we give them to him, because whatever we tell Jesus about, he makes it better, and our worries either dissolve, or we receive the power to help ourselves.

There's one huge gift that Jesus wants us to receive – and that is to trust him with our secret worries and painful habits, which are often too much for us to carry. This can take much practice and it can be helpful to keep asking God to take all this stuff away from us, because it can drag us down and make us ill. Sometimes we have days where it's fairly easy to hand over our problems, but then we have other days where we seem stuck with them! I've heard it said that, for many of us, trying to give our worries over to God is a bit like a tennis match; we tell Our Creator all about them, but can't really part from them, and so they come back to us!

I guess it's just perseverance to keep trying to live more freely without using up all our energy to worry. I read somewhere that it only takes weeks to start a bad habit, and then a lifetime to shift it! If you still find it hard to give your worries over, then keep asking God to give you the power to do this!

If you're still feeling left to it, then you may need to discover the wonder and forgiveness of Jesus. Jesus was not put off by Zacchaeus' past, it did not repel him, instead he spent his time helping Zacchaeus to turn his life round. He already knows what we've done, because we can't hide anything.

Far too many burdens and worries can make us ill

How many of us still believe that God's out to get us for everything we've done wrong?

"I'm sure God will send thunderbolts and lightning on me, because however much I try, I can't seem to overcome my unwanted habits!"

"I've made such a mess of things – has God made me ill to serve me right?"

"I can't stop worrying, and I feel left with things all the time. Can I trust Jesus to hand my problems over to? Or, will the reply be, 'You've caused it, so now you're stuck with it, so I'll make it worse for you!'"

Thinking like this all the time can really do us in. Often these thoughts come from others, so instead of believing them, we really need to question everything – if Jesus was out to get us, why did he give his life up for us? God stands ready to help you out, whatever you've done. The Creator is a friend who wants the very best for us, one where we can talk truthfully and confide about all the things that we may feel unable to tell others. Imagine inviting Jesus to sit opposite you and talk, what does it feel like? It would be loving and instructive, yes we might be told off, but this is done with a constructive divine love, rather than the failings and judgements of a human love. Jesus is closer than we could ever imagine anyway, it's just asking for our perspective to be shifted.

So who was Jesus?

Imagine turning up in a pub and suddenly noticing a young man with sunburnt and prematurely lined skin, his hair is long and unruly, there's something about the 'down and out' look that he has. It looks as though he may not have eaten for a while. He looks vulnerable, yet very powerful. There's something mysterious and compelling about him. Soon you both get into conversation, you really haven't had a good day, and you find it hard to confide in anybody, as so many people don't want to listen. So without knowing this stranger you suddenly find yourself telling him all that went wrong today – it cascades out without stopping! In fact this feels new and quite shocking; you've never done this before! Is this man going to send some barbs back?

After a while though you feel better, and then he starts to tell you about all the things that he has been doing. He's quite an activist! Always on the side of those who have been treated unfairly. He's always busy campaigning and helping, and has come in for a quiet drink, only it hasn't quite worked out like that for him. You've been busy talking about yourself, and that's OK! But it's then that you realise he has a lot to say, and he needs to talk too. You find out that he is very humble, and also clever and creative in his understanding of the world. He seems to cause controversy and misunderstandings when he turns injustices upside down in order to right them. He is involved in so much! No wonder he looks thin, doesn't look like he gets much time to eat! He seems such an ordinary guy, yet his eyes are scrutinising all, and this takes a while to get over. He's analysing you, and you can't hide! Somehow, despite this, you feel you can relax, and be yourself even though he knows about all the stuff you've done!

All of a sudden he gets up to go, he's needed! Hurriedly he finishes his drink, and dashes off a helpful remark to resolve something you've been struggling with, but haven't told anybody about. This was the one thing you held back in your conversation with him earlier, because it is a habit you're not proud of. Now he knows all about it! What a relief! His approach is down to earth yet powerful. This stranger has been good company. After he has gone you realise he's been different from anyone you have ever met. It didn't look like he agreed with everything you did and thought and that was what challenged you, but what you gained was that he held you in high regard.

You look at his empty place; there are a group of others nearby who waved when he went. It appeared they all knew him, you ask them who he was, and they reply that it was Jesus. This stranger had charisma, there was something aloof about him, yet matey, and it was obvious he liked company. As you reflect you realise how much you have gained from your chat. He was obviously the sort of person who would give everything up in order to rescue people, and you find that you have never met someone with that level of determination, commitment and dedication.

Chapter Four

Meditative Journeys!

Are You Feeling an Outcast?

They spent some time in Jericho. As Jesus was leaving town, trailed by his disciples and a parade of people, a blind beggar by the name of Bartimaeus, son of Timaeus, was sitting alongside the road. When he heard that Jesus the Nazarene was passing by, he began to cry out, "Son of David, Jesus! Mercy, have mercy on me!" Many tried to hush him up, but he yelled all the louder, "Son of David! Mercy, have mercy on me!"

Jesus stopped in his tracks. "Call him over."

They called him. "It's your lucky day! Get up! He's calling you to come!" Throwing off his coat, he was on his feet at once and came to Jesus.

Jesus said, "What can I do for you?"

The blind man said, "Rabbi, I want to see."

"On your way," said Jesus. "Your faith has saved and healed you."

In that very instant he recovered his sight and followed Jesus down the road.

(The Message)

Mark 10: 46-52

Maybe the following events happened to Bartimaeus:

Day 1 – While Bartimaeus begs by the roadside in Jericho, he hears the conversations of those around him talking about Jesus. At first Bartimaeus finds the stories he hears about Jesus far too good to be true, so while he is intrigued, he is also rather dismissive. However, when he hears about Jesus, despite his misgivings and cynicism a tiny flame suddenly ignites within him.

Day 2 – Bartimaeus is fed up with just lying on the road, begging. Those who pass by, just see him as another beggar, believing that blindness is God's curse on those who have sinned. Although God had stressed throughout the Old Testament that care was needed for those in desperate situations, the reality was, that some people did not bother to keep this commandment. Due to this ignorance, Bartimaeus was looked down on, and reviled. He had a disability, he was unable to work, and understandably he was depressed because it was all he could do to survive.

Bartimaeus knew that lying by the road in Jericho was a better place to be than other cities, simply because it was popular and the 'in' place to be. The city was appealing to many, as it had been rebuilt by Herod the Great, and was very near the Jordan River. But even though Bartimaeus constantly willed all those who were walking by to provide for him, his wishes were not happening, due to the spiritual blindness of others. Everyday just lying in the sun meant that he had little hope, and felt dehydrated, hungry, helpless, and loathed. He could feel the sun scorching his skin, and sometimes he could not find the coat that he wore as a blanket to keep him warm at night or to hide under for protection of the merciless sun, as others who were also lying by the road used it without asking him. Bartimaeus was desperate about not being able to see, and does not think he can take any more. "Why me?" he growled inside.

Day 3 – Today Bartimaeus hears a rumour that Jesus may be walking by, he feels the flame within him, which had started to ignite when he first heard the tales about Jesus, fan just a tad higher. But inside he is mocking, will he really be heard? Actually sometimes, because of his own suffering, Bartimaeus wondered if there was a God. Still he couldn't ignore the flame which even though was tiny, tried to grow inside him. Anything was worth a go, so he may as well shout out to Jesus, he reasoned. A little later on, just where Bartimaeus lies, he is aware of a large number of people who are walking along the road. Amongst them is a man's voice, which sounds healing and actually interested in those around him. That was the moment when Bartimaeus believed, despite his misgivings, and he shouted out, "Jesus, Son of David, have mercy on me!"

So many people then tell Bartimaeus to shut up! But the beggar is stronger than those in the crowd around Jesus, because he insists on not letting Jesus go, despite all the opposition of those who see themselves as so-called bodyguards around Jesus, and just want to move along. Some of the crowd with Jesus had not known desperation in the way that Bartimaeus had, and were 'blind' to the suffering of others.

Jesus though, listens to Bartimaeus, and understands; even though he knows the needs of the beggar, he humbly asks Bartimaeus what he wants him to do for him. This gives Bartimaeus a chance to speak, a time to talk, plus Jesus was waiting for the beggar to take responsibility for himself, in recognising his condition, and wanting to get better.

Suddenly Jesus commands that Bartimaeus gets up and walks over to him. Bartimaeus, in faith, then overcomes his condition and risks falling over by walking on the uneven road to Jesus. Bartimaeus can only locate Jesus by where the voice is coming from, so in this way he blindly follows. In the beggar's haste and delight he throws off his precious belonging, his coat, (the blanket), which was a prized possession in those days. It was known that people could freeze to death during cold nights without their blankets. When Bartimaeus reaches Jesus he still insists that he wants to see, and Jesus grants that. Jesus shows that, by healing the beggar, disabilities and illness aren't a curse from God for sin.

Day 4 – When Bartimaeus wakes up, he finds himself around Jesus, the disciples and the crowd of followers, having all spent the night in a sheltered dip in the desert. Upon wakening Bartimaeus celebrates, Jesus gave him perfect eyesight the day before, and the beggar still can't believe it. Bartimaeus now warms inside when some of the crowd apologise to him for regarding him as an outcast. They have all been humbled by Jesus' compassion, miracle, and merciful judgement in witnessing Jesus give the beggar his eyesight. In God's kingdom, no one is to be looked down on, or seen as not worthy.

Bartimaeus longs to stay with Jesus and his followers, but Jesus has a mission for Bartimaeus, and sends him on. The beggar has learnt more than some of the crowd, because in his faith, he kept going even through the staunch opposition from some of the followers. Bartimaeus had taken a risk. Had he got it wrong, and shouted to a group of people who were not Jesus and his followers he could have been badly beaten up. He had put his life at risk. In desperation, Bartimaeus couldn't be deterred, believing that he had nothing to lose, even when he shook off his blanket.

Bartimaeus walks along the road of Jericho waving goodbye to Jesus and the crowd. He is thankful for the new mission that Jesus has given him. Bartimaeus can now be alongside others who are suffering, and he can testify that even though we all have doubts, somehow God will bless us, when we persevere.

Two questions that Bartimaeus could ask each one of us are: "Are we recognising what God is doing in our lives? What beneficial ways or new spiritual perspectives might be happening through any depression, illness, disbelief, or cynicism?"

Rays of light are always there, even if you can't see them. Often The Holy Spirit mingles new patterns amongst any darkness we might be encountering. Can you see any new patterns which you can hang on to? If you're unsure how God may be working, try and take five or ten minutes silence out every day in quiet meditation to see.

Breakfast with Jesus

Where are you in this group? Can you imagine them?

Then the disciple Jesus loved said to Peter, "It's the Master!" When Simon Peter realized that it was the Master, he threw on some clothes, for he was stripped for work, and dove into the sea. The other disciples came in by boat for they weren't far from land, a hundred yards or so, pulling along the net full of fish. When they got out of the boat, they saw a fire laid, with fish and bread cooking on it.

Jesus said, "Bring some of the fish you've just caught." Simon Peter joined them and pulled the net to shore – 153 big fish! And even with all those fish, the net didn't rip.

Jesus said, "Breakfast is ready." Not one of the disciples dared ask, "Who are you?" They knew it was the Master.

Jesus then took the bread and gave it to them. He did the same with the fish. This was now the third time Jesus had shown himself alive to the disciples since being raised from the dead.

(The Message)

John 21: 7-14

Today the question Jesus asks you is where are you in this group?

How surprised the group must have been to have seen Jesus cooking breakfast on the beach and, he looked different even though he now had his resurrection body, they just knew it was him. This was the third time Jesus had appeared to them since rising from the dead after being crucified on the cross. Jesus' friends must have felt such relief to see him again, they knew his Holy Spirit was with them, but there's nothing like the physical, comforting bodily presence of their friend. It looks like Jesus has returned here to show his abundance and continuing friendship towards the disciples. There are so many ways to receive the infilling of the Holy Spirit, and one of the ways could be to imagine that you too, are sitting amongst the disciples. Can you taste the fish and bread? Can you feel the friendship of Jesus and those sitting with you? What is the conversation like? Can you confide while feeling the rays of the sun on you? Can you feel the warmth and understanding of Jesus and his friends with the comforting lapping of the sea behind you? Take time to imagine this realness as the days go by. My personal experience of receiving the Holy Spirit was that of feeling suddenly full, as though I had just eaten the food on offer.

The Leper

While it was still night, way before dawn, he got up and went out to a secluded spot and prayed. Simon and those with him went looking for him. They found him and said, "Everybody's looking for you."

Jesus said, "Let's go to the rest of the villages so I can preach there also. This is why I've come." He went to their meeting places all through Galilee, preaching and throwing out the demons.

A leper came to him, begging on his knees, "If you want to, you can cleanse me." Deeply moved, Jesus put out his hand, touched him, and said, "I want to. Be clean." Then and there the leprosy was gone, his skin smooth and healthy.
(The Message)
Mark 1: 35-42

A prayer of contemplation

Taking a few minutes silence everyday while thinking about the content of the Bible passages can be really beneficial, because the Holy Spirit can reveal more and more about the nature of God. Sometimes we'll realise things we never spotted before, and these insights can really help us on our way in our earthly journeys.

Jesus was often crowded by people bombarding Him with many requests. Although Jesus was fully God, he was also fully human, and he often slept rough while travelling around preaching. The disciples and others would accompany him, and while he was teaching them and helping people he must have become very exhausted, and so he would make sure that he took time out communing between himself and God, just so he could recharge and receive his instructions.

Jesus rose early that day, it was still dark and we might imagine that he was tired, and perhaps hadn't slept well that night. So, forcing his eyes open, he got up in the early hours of the morning. The sun hadn't risen yet, so there were no rays of light filtering between the trees to light his way. It was still night, and sleepily he blundered his way to a secluded place he had spotted the day before. Slowly he became more awake as he sat down to pour out how he was feeling before God. In that quietness he listened, and knew what he had to do. Jesus was enjoying his time talking with God, and he felt comforted. He wished he could have stayed far longer there, when he was suddenly interrupted by the disciples and those accompanying him. Everybody was looking for him, and by now the sun was starting to rise. It was time to start walking and moving on to Galilee to preach. There was much work to do here, as about two hundred and fifty towns could be found relatively near to each other.

Meanwhile a leper, who was ostracised by the community because they regarded leprosy sufferers as unclean, heard people shouting that they could see Jesus and his followers walking towards his town in the distance. Today, the man suffering with leprosy was feeling despair, as he had no sense of belonging anywhere. Everyone made sure of that, because, so often, rocks were thrown at him to keep him away. He was banned from any social or religious activities, and if, by chance, the religious leaders came into contact with him then they would be branded unclean too. So no one took any chances, he was left alone, and lived off scraps. The leper felt cursed.

It was late afternoon when Jesus and his followers showed up in this particular village, dust clouds gathered around their feet while they walked, everywhere was exceptionally dry. The sun was not kind that day, and everyone was far too hot. As soon as Jesus arrived, people swamped him with requests; and Jesus who had spent all the day preaching and helping others elsewhere was feeling very weary and thirsty, he really had to get some water to drink, but everywhere was so parched.

The leper knew he could not get close to Jesus as everybody would shoo him away, as though he was some sort of hated and feared predatory animal. So he waited. After a while, people left Jesus, leaving a gap for him to move forward. That was really nerve wracking for him, what if Jesus also wanted him gone, and wouldn't help him either? But then again, if Jesus really was good, then maybe he would be helped, or more than that, healed. He could only ask!

When the leper drew nearer to Jesus, he saw a tired looking man with a furrowed forehead, and a prematurely lined sunburnt face. Jesus looked so ordinary, so human and maybe vulnerable even, yet this leper had witnessed how he had healed and helped all those who were, moments ago, still clustered around him. Jesus smiled as he saw the leper walking towards him, and went out to welcome him. The leper didn't even need to explain himself, Jesus already knew of the leper's plight, and was filled with pity and compassion as well as outrage and horror because of how other people had treated this man. To Jesus it didn't matter how disfigured someone might be.

Immediately, overcome by the response of Jesus, the leper threw himself to his knees saying, "If you want to, you can cleanse me." He was really suffering with his skin, and did not feel clean himself, but he wanted much more than that, he yearned for the leprosy to be removed.

It was then that Jesus actually put out his hand and touched this man, but really it was more of a hug. The leper had forgotten what any kindness had felt like, until now. That hug did something. He felt a fire suddenly kindle within him. Jesus had said he wanted to heal this man, and so he did, and the leper received an instant healing.

What would you like Jesus to do for you? If you want to, and feel that it's relevant for you, have a go at reading this everyday for a while and keep giving over your requests. The answer's always "Yes," even if God's "Yes," is different from yours. Notice the very deep compassion and love that Jesus has for you. Nothing is too much trouble, that's what Jesus stood for. Maybe you hadn't noticed before the compassion that Jesus has for you. Homing in on that can bring about a closeness between you and Him and just focussing on that can bring about great improvements you may need for your life.

Chapter Five

Our Perceptions

Are We Seeing Everything in Our Lives as Dark and Distorted?

Are we seeing everything in our lives as dark and distorted, through a wrong perception?

Can you don a very dark pair of glasses and then look into a dirty mirror? This is a useful exercise because this can highlight how we view ourselves, our life, our circumstances and those of others in the worst possible way! Sometimes we all suffer from viewing things in the wrong way, and can have a darker perspective from the way reality is. What prejudices do we carry? What are the old habits that keep ensnaring us?

It's time to re-focus!

When we find ourselves stuck ask God to take over our minds, and ask to see everything through the eyes of divine clarity.

Spend a few moments thinking about all the people or situations in your life that are distressing you – give them over, ask for clarity and ask for new ways of seeing things. Also be honest with yourself in a kind way! Have you done anything to inflame a situation? If you have, ask God how you can make it better. Take as much time as you need and see if you can gain other, new perspectives. Make notes on bits of paper so you can look at your insights.

Looking at yourself through the dark glasses in the mirror you will notice that your image will be dimmed, this just shows what it's like living with a distorted viewpoint! It stops clarity and can cause much distress, often when there needn't be! What can you do to help yourself alongside the help of God?

A Journey into Peace

"I'm leaving you well and whole. That's my parting gift to you. Peace. I don't leave you the way you're used to being left – feeling abandoned, bereft. So don't be upset. Don't be distraught."
(The Message)
John 14: 27

"Don't be upset. Don't be distraught." Not easy! We'll always live with broken dreams, and realise that life is at times not the way we would want it! This is hard. We all need a time of reflection, and a time to mourn, but there's also times where healing mingles and sheds light on the difficult times. Sometimes we'll also need to distract ourselves with a hobby, music or TV programme, away from what is going on in the world around us. Life in this world will always be like this, bittersweet. We are wounded, yet we are healed at the same time, otherwise we would not be able to live the lives we are living. When we remain stuck in a time where we feel everything is against us, it's a good idea to ask Jesus to help us look at the situation, to review it through his eyes, and then to turn us away from our fears; to turn us from imagining that we can't cope, to believing that we can. Just affirming that God is there and on our side will help turn our thoughts around to being more manageable and positive. Peace is always there, at times it seems beyond our grasp, but it is there to discover. Peace is a spiritual gift offered to all and is beyond anything that the world can offer us. If we trust God we can offer up the situations we don't want, and ask to see the scenarios from an aerial view, rather than from our own perspectives. We might after all be trying to force our own agendas into situations which aren't right! Life is always a puzzle and is often beyond our control. This is when we need to affirm that we always have a friend who won't fail us, and will always protect us. Jesus will always lead us through the darkness and sadness to light and peace. Trust always!

Chapter Six

Oh! It's Christmas!

So Many of Us Are Desperately Seeking and Searching

"God's kingdom is like a treasure hidden in a field for years and then accidently found by a trespasser. The finder is ecstatic – what a find! – and proceeds to sell everything he owns to raise money and buy that field.

"Or, God's kingdom is like a jewel merchant on the hunt for excellent pearls. Finding one that is flawless, he immediately sells everything and buys it."

(The Message)

Matthew 13: 44-46

How we can find God's love and blessing – the pearl of great treasure, this Christmas

So many of us are desperately seeking and searching for something. This search is as though we are trawling through a muddy field, sinking up to our knees in the mire, while we look for what we've been searching for. As we walk with our knees sinking in the mud, we might become aware that we're hunting for treasures such as God's love and blessings amongst the complexities of life. We often walk through the mud when we've lost our way, and for a while we cannot find our way to any helpful signposts, which may just be the keys to the treasure we are seeking.

This doesn't necessarily mean a worldly sense of treasure, although we all need enough to pay our bills, I guess we're all looking for a sense of reassurance, unconditional love, and a sense of any loneliness we feel to be replaced by a deep companionship, where we can relax, be who we are, and never feel the need to explain ourselves. We may be searching for God in many different ways, and once we find that priceless treasure amongst the muddy field we bring our losses, our sadness, the things that bring us down, the prayers we feel have never been answered, and in the middle of our temporary darkness we suddenly see the pearl (Jesus) glistening in our desperate search. We all want and need something that we don't have at the moment.

Christmas is a time which the adverts tell us will consist of compulsory fun. It's all presented with smiling relatives or friends sitting around a Christmas feast with huge amounts of food on the table. While some people adore Christmas and have truly happy families, so many others do not. It's easy to go out shopping and watch the passers by, believing that everyone else has got it made, and their lives are perfect. But that's not the case for most people. We never know what traumas they're hiding underneath a smiling face.

Whatever happens during your Christmas, don't lose yourself underneath all that's going on. If you have family or friends, they are a gift, and security in one sense, but no one can give us every-thing we need. It's so important not to live our lives "automati-cally" through others. We can rely on others to some extent, but they too will come and go, because they have their own lives to lead and their own unmet wants and needs to find that sometimes we can't provide, try as we might.

It can be easy to see God as an added on extra bit of security after our friends and families. Even though people in our lives are incredibly valuable, they can, at times, distract us away from our times with God. We all come into this world alone. Everything else in our lives is a gift, which is much to be thankful for, but it can clutter up and cover over our divine link, a bit like a heavy snowfall.

It's times like Christmas which cause us to mull over the hardships and busyness of our lives. Some of us will be spending Christmas alone, and could be feeling miserable, or elated over it!

Or even if you're part of a big family, you can still have a sense of loneliness at times. All our losses and crises lead us to God who has watched over our lives, even if we may query this at times!

Underneath all our lives there's a faithful friend who will never go, or leave us, it's a friend who has the unconditional love for each one of us. If you find yourself alone this Christmas, just remembering that Jesus is Emmanuel (God with us), will bring that presence and blessing closer. It can take a while to find God's companionship in the loneliness or traumas, but our Creator is waiting to be found, because our suffering highlights the need for God. In this search you won't be let down, you will be blessed in some sense, because when things are hard, Jesus comes to the rescue in a way which others often can't! He is The Pearl of Great Value and is with us permanently whereas our family and friends have their own journeys to make. May God's love and peace be born in you over Christmas – the greatest gifts anyone could own. When everything else is stripped away Jesus is there!

What Would Jesus Say to You in a Christmas Card Sent to You?

Take time out to reflect what Jesus would say to you in a Christmas card sent from him to you! How has the year gone for you? What are your hopes and disappointments? Is there anything you've learned when life hasn't gone the way you've wanted it to? What is that saying to you? Whatever you feel – God's feedback is always constructive, and not delivered in critical ways which is how the world does it.

Before you make a Christmas card to yourself from Jesus, do you have a sense of what he may be saying? Sometimes people may get a picture in their heads, or they might feel something, while others may have had a recent and continuing message from other people which is helpful and can often be from God. Others may receive a sudden beneficial idea in their minds, whilst others may have had a God dream. Everyone hears in a completely different way; if you don't hear anything, that doesn't matter, as you can't rush it. We are all equally loved, so don't compare yourself! Often Our Creator reveals things in total quietness.

Now make and decorate that Christmas card from Jesus to yourself!

Christmas can often be a hard time to get through

For some people Christmas is the most traumatic time of the year, if this is you, then please pray about it and ask God to help you through it. Is there anything different you can do this Christmas? What do you think Jesus may be saying to you about this? The build-up that goes on in the shops and in the adverts on TV doesn't help those, who, for many reasons, may not enjoy this time of year. For those going through a difficult time the best thing is not to get sucked into the way the media portrays Christmas as it's only done to sell products. The reality of Christmas is about light coming into our own darkness and transforming it, which is what Jesus stood for when he came into this world. I always remember a particular friend of mine who had a large family – many would assume she had it all, but one day she said, 'we can have many people around us, but we can still be lonely, and that's me'. None of us really know how others live their lives, and none of us know what is missing from other people's lives either.

Christmas is a time of anticipation and transformation, regardless of how we spend the season. If you can, try and make the light of God the centre point in your thoughts and ask for divine power to take you through the season in the way that Jesus would like you to spend Christmas. You may be in for a few surprises! Christmas can be one of those times where we can ask the Holy Spirit to be born in us, so that we can anticipate our lives transforming in many ways of blessing. Some of us may be alone, but none of us are really alone as God is always with us. It's just asking Jesus to give us the sense of shared companionship with him, so that we can feel the comfort around us. How we spend Christmas will be unique for each one of us.

Anticipation of the Holy Spirit being born in you can happen at any point, it's all down to God's timing. These verses may prepare you for a comforting transformation

In the sixth month of Elizabeth's pregnancy, God sent the angel Gabriel to the Galilean village of Nazareth to a virgin engaged to be married to a man descended from David. His name was Joseph, and the virgin's name, Mary. Upon entering, Gabriel greeted her:

Good morning!
You're beautiful with God's beauty,
Beautiful inside and out!
God be with you.

She was thoroughly shaken, wondering what was behind a greeting like that. But the angel assured her, "Mary, you have nothing to fear. God has a surprise for you: You will become pregnant and give birth to a son and call his name Jesus."
(The Message)
Luke 1: 26-33

God's Promise of Hope – Despite Carrying Any Inner Wounds

Do you bear any inner wounds? This can happen when we get badly hurt, or bereaved. If you feel this applies to you, please pray for an inner healing, while asking yourself why the wound is there?

Consider the passage from Luke shown below, which tells of

the encounter between Joseph and Mary and Simeon on the occasion of the presentation of the infant Jesus at the temple. (Simeon was an elderly man who had been promised by the Holy Spirit that he would see the Messiah before he died.) So, whilst recognizing the joy that the Messiah has come, it also foretells the hurt that Mary will suffer when her son fulfils his mission in his crucifixion.

**Simeon went on to bless them, and said to Mary his [Jesus']
mother,**

**This child marks both the failure and
the recovery of many in Israel,
A figure misunderstood and contradicted -
the pain of a sword-thrust through you -
But the rejection will force honesty,
as God reveals who they really are.**
(The Message)
Luke 2: 34-35

If you have the wound of a sword piercing your soul, you may feel an inner pain which is not physical, but spiritual. This wound can happen at times of great distress and very deep pain. For me, I felt my soul rip into two halves inside me when I was encountering bereavement as a child. This pain like any physical wound can be felt. When this wound had fulfilled its purpose for me, it was really hard work to overcome it. I did remember being told by The Holy Spirit at the time of the wound that 'my vocation would come out of my wound.' In other words, God, I believe, had baptised me into a service of helping the marginalised, and those going through loss in some way. Everything has a purpose even though none of us want suffering.

Eventually after a season of distress, I do believe a time of consolation arrives where we find that God wants to help us out of it, because the wound has served its vocation, and we finally need a rest from all the distress it caused us. The consolation time heralds new ways of being where God reaches out and provides help and rescue in the most unexpected ways! Anticipation of greater, better things for our lives and the unexpected can work together. Whether we are with families and friends, or without, we are never alone when we have with us the perfect Father or Mother (however you name God). Whenever we feel alone, lost, or without friends, God can provide comfort and guidance. What is distressing one minute, can transform from darkness to light showing gold tinges. God is always working within us. It's making sure that we take time to listen to help ourselves manage a better life, as we co-operate with the workings of divine help and rescue.

Chapter Seven

Your Future with God

Plans for Your Future

"I know what I'm doing. I have it all planned out – plans to take care of you, not abandon you, plans to give you the future you hope for.

"When you call on me, when you come and pray to me, I'll listen.

"When you come looking for me, you'll find me.

"Yes, when you get serious about finding me and want it more than anything else, I'll make sure you won't be disappointed." GOD'S Decree.

(The Message)

Jeremiah 29: 11-14

Time to prepare good lives for ourselves

A new year has started! It doesn't necessarily mean though that we automatically start new lives. It all depends on what spiritual season we find ourselves in. There are times when life is really hard, and everything takes an effort as we struggle with many issues and challenges that suddenly come at us. Sometimes we might even wonder what is going on. It can seem as though we have been plunged into a barren wasteland with withering trees which represent how we feel during this time of burnout and trials. Am I going to stay in this difficult place forever, you might ask?

We could even think that the rest of our life will also be a continuation of the same trial. Often though, life starts to improve after a time of hardship when characteristics we didn't know we had, suddenly spring up in us to aid us through these hard times, and our strengths appear in the forms of resilience, endurance, perseverance, greater compassion and patience! The good news is that those characteristics are now here to stay, and the hard times in our lives are allowed for us to give birth to greater persistence and character. Now these newly formed characteristics will see us through the rest of our lives, and all of these came into being when we needed them. How strong each one of us is! (Even if you still doubt yourself, you've still got through.) We are all like flowers, bits are pruned back that either don't serve us, or our branches are pruned back to produce even greater blooms. Hard times in life are about great growth.

All of a sudden though, life changes and the hardships melt into a time of blessing, our barren wasteland with withering trees transforms itself into a landscape of greenery, flowers and newness, (even though some difficult situations might remain unchanged). The Holy Spirit always goes on before us preparing the way, but it can be so easy sometimes to remain stuck in the hard times and not reach the time of great blessings when they appear – which they always do.

If you can, try and have times of silence everyday after asking God to show you what season you are in. There's always another perspective on everything. Just having five to ten minutes of asking a question then trying to be quiet and listen can change everything – it's a mini retreat. If you can give more time then that could also be helpful for you. Something is always revealed in the stillness – a useful thought, a picture in your head, clarity, or just feeling better, etc. Sometimes, this is when the Holy Spirit can bring things out to heal. If, however, you feel you need some professional guidance for the thoughts that arise, then it is advisable to seek out a trusted and qualified person to help; the skills of others can work alongside God's healing.

Our lives are all tapestries – there are beautiful woven threads of gold in the pictures we weave in our lives. Alongside the lavish gold threads can be dark, black threads of suffering. But it's so vital to just live, however you're feeling, and create the best life you can for yourself to bring in extra light, (the gold amongst the black). Start to treasure yourself as a best friend, meet up with your friends more often, and go after that hobby. Try new interests. Just living and looking for things to thank God for everyday (no matter how small) can ease a sense of loss and sadness. Each of our lives are tailored for ourselves, it's easy to compare our own lives with other people's and believe they have it better than us, whereas we have blessings to celebrate too.

God always promises a better future, no matter what we're feeling or going through. In contrast with earthly promises – God's ones always come true, it's just a matter of making sure we see what's going on, and go with the flow of blessings and opportunities. It can be easy to fight against what suddenly opens up for us in a disguise of a blessing, and resist what plans God has for us. But if we just stop and see what this blessing can lead to it helps to surrender, and go with what God's already planned. It's helpful to look at your life and keep a journal and note all the new things that have come up for you. Is there a thread of a new, better direction in everything that has been happening for you? Or have there been a series of signposts warning you away from the season you were in, to new greater things. Change is the only constant, and it doesn't necessarily have to be scary. When you know life is changing for the better, which it always eventually does, then go with it, and receive greater blessings. (God always plans better things than we ever could for ourselves, it's all tailored to suit our gifts and personalities, and the blessings always fit our lives perfectly, even if we may at first wonder what is going on.)

When any plans we might have made for ourselves don't work out, or are blocked – The Creator's not being a killjoy – it's all about opening new, better doors of blessing for you, and these are inviting and imploring us to travel through them. Enter the better life; it's all been prepared just for you!

Thoughts for a New Year. Can We Ask God's Help to Make Any Beneficial Changes?

Putting our inner worlds right, how to fly freely

Sunday – "The place where your treasure is, is the place you will most want to be, and end up being."
What is the treasure inside you which you can use to help others? Everyone has unique gifts. Dear Jesus, let me not doubt my gifts, please make sure that I use them, by prompting me to ask you everyday, "How can I help you today?"

Monday – "... and don't get worked up about what may or may not happen tomorrow. God will help you deal with whatever hard things come up when the time comes." Or put another way –
Help me Lord, you already know what's going to meet me tomorrow, as your power has already gone ahead, so help me not to worry, and to let go and trust in your power instead.

Tuesday – "Your eyes are windows into your body. If you open your eyes wide in wonder and belief, your body fills up with light."
Dear Jesus please help me to stop thinking about my heavy burdens all the time, so that your light and healing will sort them out for me.

Wednesday – "If you pull the blinds on your windows, what a dark life you will have!" *Is there something you don't want to face, and have walked away from after giving up? Dear Jesus help me to realise that we have victory in your strength so that I can overcome in your power.*

Thursday – "If you decide for God, living a life of God-worship, it follows that you don't fuss about what's on the table

at mealtimes or whether the clothes in your closet are in fashion."

Dear Jesus the world sometimes contaminates my mind with clutter and wants, help me to simplify my life, and find my path once again.

Friday – "There is far more to your life than the food you put in your stomach, more to your outer appearance than the clothes you hang on your body."

Dear Jesus, help me not to compare myself to others, as we are all beautiful because you created us!

Saturday – "Look at the birds, free and unfettered, not tied down to a job description, careless in the care of God."

Dear Jesus in this world people are introduced by what job they do, as people crave titles for their self-worth. Help me to live as a responsible free spirit and show the belief in myself which I have from you, which can do away with titles.

Sunday – "And you count far more to him than birds." The divine trinity loves us more than we could ever take in.

Dear Jesus please be at the centre of my mind, so that I can take in the vitality of your love.

Monday – "Has anyone by fussing in front of the mirror ever gotten taller by so much as an inch?"

Dear Jesus, please heal my worry habit, and help me to talk more kindly to myself so that I can nurture myself, which both eases my worries and co-operates with your help to heal habits I don't want.

Tuesday – "Instead of looking at the fashions, walk out into the fields and look at the wildflowers."

Dear Jesus, help me to receive the restorative nature of your creation.

Wednesday – "They [the wildflowers] never primp or shop, but

have you ever seen color and design quite like it?"

Dear Jesus, please release me from striving, and expand my mind beyond my own world of conflicting thoughts, so that I can see who or what you need me to pray for in the world.

Thursday – "The ten best-dressed men and women in the country look shabby alongside them [the wildflowers]!" – God promises to provide for our needs. Can we donate any good clothes to a homeless charity, so people on the street can regain their dignity?

Dear Jesus, Please give the homeless employment, a time to thrive and with that let them burst into beauty and bloom with your provision.

Friday – "If God gives such attention to the appearance of wildflowers – most of which are never even seen – don't you think he'll attend to you, take pride in you, do his best for you?"

Hey, Jesus, you know that shopping list of my needs, you still haven't answered them! Help me to move on from these, so that I can receive your greater blessings, as you already know my needs!

Saturday – "What I'm trying to do here is to get you to relax, to not be so preoccupied with *getting* so you can respond to God's giving."

Hey Jesus, I'm back to insisting that you provide my shopping list of needs and wants again! Help me to relax, and just live, so that I can respond to your generosity.

Sunday – The birds outside our windows, feed, bathe, nest, fly, and soar to great heights. At some level it is as though they know the Divine has responsibility for them, because they don't worry.

Dear Jesus, I too want to soar, as though I too am flying, lightly in your power, but at the moment this seems impossible for me. Help me to rise to new heights, and make what was once impossible for me to achieve, now possible. Help me to see you in a huge perfect light and know that you are responsible for me; it's not up to me alone! Please grant me clarity to see your guardianship of me anew.

Monday – "People who don't know God and the way he works fuss over these things, but you know both God and how he works."

Dear Jesus, please release me from once again fussing over my shopping list about my urgent needs and wants, and let me live freely and lightly so that I can soar into new heights of faith, and fly!

Tuesday – "Steep your life in God-reality, God initiative, God-provisions. Don't worry about missing out. You'll find all your everyday human concerns will be met."

Dear Jesus, I need both some help and advice today. Please send the right people into my life, and let me receive their help, which will bless both their gifts, and my asking. You provide extra light when life is dark!

Wednesday – "Give your entire attention to what God is doing right now,"

Dear Jesus let me live in the present with you, and please heal my memories of hurtful situations so that they don't keep going round my mind.

How we can put into practice Matthew 6: 19 – 34

Thursday – *Dear Jesus, that person really got to me, and I'm finding it hard to forgive. I notice that wild birds have initial squabbles over food or territories, then they let go, and fly on. Let me do the same.*

Friday – *Dear Jesus, help me to imagine what it is to be like another person, so that I may understand what they are trying to say. Please give me greater compassion and insight, so that I can see beyond*

anything causative in my life or theirs which could sully my friend-
ships.

Saturday – *Dear Jesus, sometimes I'm not really sure who my friends
are, or who I can trust, as I've been hurt before, please show me who my
real friends are! Please help me not to become depressed over this. I
would really like the gift of holy laughter, which is both cleansing,
healing, and laughs with people and not at them. Help me to give others
extra light, and not to take life too seriously, because I really need a
release and haven't laughed for ages!*

Sunday – Practical Joke Day! *Dear Jesus, I feel joyless, yet you offer
joy, I need some light, some laughter once again as you make my real
friends clear to me. Help me to play an appropriate, non-offensive
practical joke today on someone who could take it, so that they will
laugh, and forget their upsetting situations too!*

Monday – It's that Monday morning feeling! *Dear Jesus I woke up
groaning about Monday, please turn this around by helping me to pray
and meditate for your perspectives on life! The great thing is that I'm
alive and that you have better plans for me!*

Tuesday – *Dear Jesus, please give me today the spirit of adventure,
whether I'm at home, outdoors, or at work, etc. Is there anything I can
do to help anybody? If there is, either put them in my mind to pray for,
or help me to help them. Could you also lead me into a new experience
that I can benefit from, as adventures can happen around us at any time,
and I just need a taste of the unknown!*

Wednesday – *Dear Jesus, the world often presents dark and negative
thoughts. Please help me to see through these illusions, to either learn
from them, or dismiss them, and free others.*

Thursday – *Dear Jesus, help me to keep realising that prayers are* *answered in your own way, not in the way I would solve the problems in my life. Also, please let me keep recognising that positive or helpful repetitive messages which echo in my thoughts are often from you, giving me direction and help.*

Friday – *Dear Jesus, help me to listen to the feelings within me so that I can live both freely and safely. Help me to listen to both warning feelings, and safe feelings, so that I know which situations and people are right for my life, so that I don't invite distress. Ta, for your satnav!*

Saturday – *Dear Jesus, please encourage my treasure within to shine today, so that I can encourage others in their gifts. The world is so keen to put people down, let me build others up, so they can achieve great blessings for their lives.*

Sunday – *Dear Jesus, there's so much injustice in the world with people suffering in war zones, so that they are unable to fly. I pray for peace, forgiveness and justice, starting with myself.*

Monday – *Dear Jesus, it's that Monday morning feeling again! So often the sunshine and blue skies I find in the summer, often disappear in the winter. Please let your love, like the warmth of the sun, remain deep within me, so that the blue sky effect will always keep your joy deep within me, whatever the weather.*

(The Message)
Extracts from Matthew 6: 19-34

Chapter Eight

Healing Strategies

Suggestions for healing strategies

God can heal in a myriad of ways, tailor made for each person, there's no formula. Sometimes it's hunting for keys to unlock our healing, such as therapies, medication, counselling if needed. It takes great courage to face self; it's not a soft option! Often all this helps towards the healing, whatever it is that we need.

Sometimes what we want removed from our life could remain if it furthers that person's life mission. For example, Paul in his second letter to the Corinthians tells of an affliction which he struggled with greatly, and repeatedly asked God to heal, but it continued to play a part in his life.

At first I didn't think of it as a gift, and begged God to remove it. Three times I did that, and then he told me,

My grace is enough; it's all you need.
My strength comes into its own in your weakness.
(The Message)
2 Corinthians 12:8-9

It's OK to express how you feel to God!

Don't despair! When you really get fed up with a medical condition, or a burden, etc., it's so important to tell God how you really feel, and if you're angry say it! Often God shifts something from your situation when you feel you can't cope with what's going on.

Some reflections to help you through

There's always another perspective – what does God want you to learn from it? I realised it was important to ask this question, because sometimes illnesses remain to teach, and enhance spiritual growth.

Often there is a life-cycle of an illness, sometimes it can be overcome, by living a life and managing the health problem with medication, and trying to do the best you can. Self-pity can emerge now and again, but becoming a 'victim,' to your condition could prolong the life of it. I believe that when we need a miracle God asks us to co-operate, so we pray and try and live, by reframing some of our thoughts, while still thinking realistically, so we don't repress anything!

Although I was eventually healed from a life-long lung condition, the years I suffered from it helped me to develop wisdom. Having to organise a life, and learning how to live, while managing an illness with medication needs much thought, preparation and courage! During my childhood I never knew if I would survive or not, and was on a multitude of medication to keep me going. Sometimes I was too ill to walk, and because of this I would pray and meditate and despite shouting at God in anger, I became much closer to The Creator and realised that God was calling me to be a friend. This is because I did not have the health to run away from God! So, from this, I learnt who I was!

Often it helps to keep saying 'I receive my healing,' to reinforce your openness to healing – whilst still recognising that it's in God's hands. I believe we get the healing we need, even though it might come in another form we don't agree with. God goes before us, knowing what's needed.

You might want to keep a spiritual journal – and write everyday: the blessings, things to be happy about, overwhelming worries, and observe and record over the future days how all this is sorted out. Give time to Jesus in prayer and contemplation everyday, the more you write down, the more you will receive.

Is your illness remaining because it is protecting you from facing the harsh realities of your life? Sometimes our illnesses are here, with the best intention of protecting us from the world, a place where we feel we cannot cope. Have you asked your illness why it is there? You may be surprised at the reply, when we listen, we may understand.

Some people have taken the view that illnesses have a consciousness, and we have been given authority to ask them to leave us. Doing this in combination with my faith in God's power to heal is what helped me. All the results though are in God's hands, it's just trying to co-operate with what God might ask you to do. Don't worry if what you want removed still remains, God will bless you in some other way.

Do you still want to get better? In the passage of John 5: 6 about the pool called Bethesda – people believed that when the pool was stirred, the ill ones had to immediately immerse themselves, because an angel of healing had made the ripples on the water ready to heal the next person. Jesus coming across a man who had been an invalid there for thirty-eight years, asked him how long he had been there, and did he want to get well? The man procrastinated.

The sick man said, "Sir, when the water is stirred, I don't have anybody to put me in the pool. By the time I get there, somebody else is already in."
(The Message)
John 5: 7

There are many different ways to analyse his reply. It could be a message about self-pity, and giving up on getting better and being healed; sometimes we have to help ourselves in order to co-operate with God's healing. It looks like this man was stuck, but at least he had displayed the co-operation to remain by the pool. When health improves we need to be ready to shed any comfort habits we have made during our illness that won't serve us when we are well and may well hinder our new life of health. Some of them may be negative comfort habits – such as not wanting to take part in real life again because we find it easier not to!

The many ways in which prayers can be answered

Sometimes our prayers are answered in our minds! We suddenly know something, we feel an inner wisdom. Listen to how you feel – if you feel a great disturbance within, often it's an 'alarm system,' warning you to act in a health situation, or telling you how to avoid a forthcoming event which could harm you, or when you feel something is right, you can feel an inner 'Yes.'

Our prayers are also answered by various people suddenly giving us the same message! God's trying to tell you something here! Others will receive messages that highlight themselves in the Bible or elsewhere! People can have God dreams that are far more real than any other dreams. Visions such as positive pictures can appear in the mind, and angels can intervene in rescuing us. Even if none of these things happen – you may be aware of how an insoluble situation has suddenly changed to one of becoming more manageable through the unseen, but sure workings of the divine!

Answers to our prayers take place in many ways! God shows each of us unconditional love in a personal way through our thoughts, beliefs, perspectives, actions, responses, dreams, hobbies, gifts, friends, goals and life experiences. We all process information in different ways, and this is how God gets our personal attention and talks to us so that we can receive the help we need from our prayers.

Do you know who you are?

Love yourself; get to know who you are. Often I think it's sad for those at the end of their lives who have never appreciated the specialness of who they are, because they have never got to know themselves. They may instead have believed the untrue and unkind criticisms of others. This can smother a beautiful person's light as though they are covered with a heavy black blanket. What are the lies that you believe are true about you? What is the evidence? Lies are no evidence; they come from a dark perspective. Constructive feedback though, is aimed to help, and is in a completely different realm to untruths.

How would you cope with a sudden recovery from illness?

A sudden recovery from an illness can mean that other people spring their busy plans on us, in a way they couldn't do when we were ill! It is so easy to get caught up in this, and we can find ourselves suddenly very tired with helping in areas we are not gifted in, or called to. Don't lose your newly regained health; you may need time to adjust to your new life, before you do anything! How will you cope with other people's demands, can you say 'no,' without feeling guilty, while remaining true to the cause you are called to help with?

If you suddenly start to regain good health while those you have been praying about are still not well, don't feel guilty about your recovery, divine healing is a mystery, and we cannot change how God works. So much is out of our control!

Are your prayers just a shopping list?

Is your relationship with God only based on a shopping list? Jesus came to be our personal friend; can you try and be a friend back? How would you feel if a person kept demanding that you do things for them, while they didn't respect or want to know you? God asks us for a real relationship, and this is a positive starting place.

On seeing the suffering around us in the world

Try and focus on divine compassion, rather than all the wrong around you. Tragic disasters can happen; we see them on the news every day. It doesn't help to think God doesn't care, or doesn't want to know what's wrong with you. Some people even think God is not strong enough to heal or can't be everywhere, because it's a big world, and that's impossible! Try and look at your own blessings, rather than take on all the trouble in the world! At the same time though, focus on a social conscience about world matters, pray about them, but don't torture yourself about stuff in the newspapers or it can pull you down.

Loving yourself

Loving yourself can take time. Look in the mirror and see if you welcome or refuse yourself. What issues do you own? What have others put upon you? Ask to see through God's eyes, to clear anything away which has been clouding the view you have of yourself. When we refuse to accept ourselves we are denying that we are made in God's Image. Can you learn to welcome you?

Reframe your thoughts towards self and others more kindly, and nurture yourself as if you are looking after a child! Ask God to be at the centre of your mind. Even when we slip up, there's no need to reject ourselves.

My dear children, let's not just talk about love; let's practice real love. This is the only way we'll know we're living truly, living in God's reality. It's also the way to shut down debilitating self-criticism, even when there is something to it. For God is greater than our worried hearts and knows more about us than we do ourselves.
(The Message)
1 John 3: 18-20

Looking at yourself – why do you react the way you do?

Analyse your conscience everyday! If there's anything you've done wrong, tell God, and talk it out. Give thanks, look for other perspectives; go within yourself. Is there anything hindering your healing, like unforgiveness? We can't stop what others do to us, but we can stop feeling bitter, and consequently taking it out on the rest of the people we meet!

What reactions do you have? Why do you feel this way over certain circumstances? Once again it is helpful to know your triggers, so that God can heal and work with you during this time. Are you projecting any of your own stuff onto others? God's promise is for wholeness, even if for some it works out to be a spiritual healing, rather than any healing given for a physical health problem.

Challenge yourself!

Expand your mind – often the Holy Spirit will teach us and take us beyond where we are now. This can be especially painful, if at first, we cannot reach where we are aiming for. Not being able to let go can be one of those habits which are hindering our progress. It takes a sudden burst of courage to let go of habits, so ask for the courage you need to overcome. Are you really seeking after God?

Being with God

Can you surrender everything to God to help you find your future spiritual path?

Ask the Holy Spirit how much prayer time to give everyday, and try and keep it.

Being with God is just another relationship to spare time for; it's all about being saved from ourselves!

Trust the divine promises!

God always keeps divine promises, and they often happen in a different time frame from ours! I've always wanted the promises now! But I've often had to wait and that has made me learn a bit of patience! But some miracles are instant.

Miracles abound everyday if you look for them! Even if they are ones we haven't asked for! We have at least woken up breathing!

Common experiences that so many people share

When you are struggling with unwanted thoughts or temptations – can you stick up for yourself and answer them back with authority? Practise! Don't over identify with distressing thoughts. Tell them they are not you, and that you are not scared of them, that they are lies! If you need professional help to get better, it's wise to accept that too. Help is always there.

Soul ties!

What are these? Soul ties are present when you feel bound to, or by, someone in a web of unforgiveness, and you simply can't let go of them. There may also be a feeling of being entangled with your family history or a person. We can also cause soul ties by being unable to let go of unwanted habits which we hate, but don't know how to shift or overcome. When we are suffering from soul ties some of these situations remain and impact upon our thoughts and health, and we feel at the mercy of them. Ask Jesus to cut all your soul ties and He will set you free as you forgive all those in your ancestry, or who have bound themselves to you, or forgive yourself for binding yourself to another. This takes time, and it's helpful to imagine ropes or chains being cut! This is very common, you are not alone! Sometimes family memories are passed down through generations in many ways such as illnesses, behaviours and habits. Once again ask for your soul ties to be cut, but beware, do not keep delving, or become obsessed about this!

Forgiveness

Forgiveness – are you carrying grudges? How heavy that is! It's sometimes really hard to forgive anyone who has purposely hurt you – but most of us offend people without knowing. (How horrified we would be if we realised we had unknowingly hurt someone.) Forgiveness is about letting go of your own harmful feelings towards another. You don't want to become like the person who's purposely hurt you! Sometimes we are hurt through people not being aware of their own issues and the wounds they are working out of. To keep hold of unforgiveness means that you are continually trapped with the other person, although they may no longer be in your life. When we forgive we not only release ourselves, but also the other person. It doesn't mean that what they did was fine and OK, it means that what happened was not OK, but we're going to find the will to let go and start living. There's a freedom to this; holding onto unwanted stuff is like continually wearing a heavy stained overcoat, which we don't want to wear, but find that it's become a habit. Ask God to help you forgive – sometimes that extra special help is what is needed! Also let your self-esteem rise, when we think more of ourselves, we find it easier to forgive others when they slip up! When you're able to forgive, life becomes lighter, and you regain a renewed, happier energy.

Protection and comfort

God has ordered his angels to care for us; we are never spiritually abandoned, even though we may feel like it, read Psalm 91! Bereavement and grieving can especially make us feel cut off from everyone else. But, the reality is that God always works behind the scenes in ways we don't know of.

When we feel alone it can help to keep affirming that God is present around us and within us, it can change your view of being left to it!

Time out, stop!

There are times we need just for ourselves, when our health is too poor to do anything else. Please be aware of this, and don't force yourself to keep helping others when you aren't able to do this. Sometimes it's vital just to be there for you.

Perseverance and outcomes

Don't give up if you're fed up with waiting for a situation to improve. Waiting can enhance endurance and perseverance and build your character to become more resilient, but none of us want to wait and wait! Don't give up, when you could be so near. A relationship with God is like any other friendship there's always issues, but it's important to keep going, even when you feel as though you've lost heart, let God know all about it, don't repress or hide anything because that can be cleared away to reach newness.

Common experiences of past traumas that appear to cling on

Do you find yourself often reliving an upsetting event from the past (possibly during childhood)? When you think about it, do you return to the age and emotions you were when it happened? Momentarily you may experience the powerlessness of the child you were. If you are an adult now, how can you look at it without perpetually experiencing this powerlessness? Sometimes traumas last until they are ready to go. What has it taught you? Can you understand it from another perspective? Do you need to keep entering this area, what are the triggers that occur which pull you down into it? Can you find a new way ahead with the wisdom you have learnt since then to be in control of it? How has it influenced your life? This does not excuse what happened, but it might be helpful to imagine that Jesus is holding a box for you to place this in so he can redeem it.

If you've been praying for someone's healing and they die – that is not your fault

If you are praying for someone's healing and they die, that is not up to you. It could be that death will provide the healing that they need. Very painful – but you have not caused their demise.

Medication

Don't suddenly come off any prescribed medication after prayers for healing, as they aid God's healing. Medication is here for a reason, it can save lives! Faith doesn't demand that you make yourself seriously ill by taking risks in this way, God's healing for us comes in many ways, and not always the ways we want. We have faith in taking medication, so we can get well! If your health suddenly becomes dramatically better, please see your doctor to make a plan ahead.

Illnesses can leave memories inside the body and because the body has been used to working a certain way with whatever is afflicting you, it does not know how to work as a well body. Keep affirming you are well even if you have to go to the doctor or hospital for a time of poor health, it is no shame if you need extra medication – take it! But by repeatedly affirming you are well, whilst acknowledging your illness, stops you concentrating on feeling ill all the time and the body may start to re-programme itself to become better.

If you suddenly notice your health vastly improving or even if you believe that your illness has been removed – beware! An imprint of the illness can still remain because the body, mind and spirit can hold onto the memories of it, and you may find that what once afflicted you can still make sudden, unwanted reappearances! Please make sure that you keep hold of your medication, because you may still need it! Once again, please make sure you see your doctor, and don't come off medication without their agreement!

Fitness

Fitness – exercise, diet, having respect, looking after yourself and making more time for you – also prepares the body for sounder health. But keep within the limitations that your body can achieve, do not push yourself under any circumstances.

Learning from our experience

Look at the past to learn from it, but don't live in it, embrace the present. The past is a country that is now far away! Learn how to receive peace from God. There are always new spiritual tools that come to us to help us move on.

Chapter Nine

A New Destination

A Turbulent Journey, What a Struggle!

God often brings things out in order to heal them! Those nightmarish events which we want to avoid, we suddenly have to face, as a storm brews in our lives! So often this is divine intervention. It is turbulent, nothing seems safe, our whole world is shaken, and we find that we can't hide! During this time of being shaken up, all the stuff that destroys us inside our minds and in our lives starts to come up.

You are ready to board for a new destination, but can you leave your baggage behind?

You are struggling to let go of your conflicts, and bravely in one split second you pack your past baggage inside your holiday suitcases and leave them behind. Now you are preparing to travel to your new destination which is a higher place in your soul. After relinquishing the stuff that destroys, you feel very free and joyful, life has never felt so good, but then what do you do? You grab that baggage back! 'No, I can't let it go?' 'Why not?' For many of us there is a strange familiarity in holding onto what we know, but we need more than a brief holiday from them, only to return and find ourselves back to our old wounds and ways. What we need is to move on permanently and risk leaving the past! That risk is a big fear factor for some of us!

Spiritual promotion often works with turbulence! It's the other side; it's what comes out of being shaken up! Jesus is there standing at the departure gate. He wants you to board, to dump your baggage, and travel to your new destination which is onto a higher place. Are you ready for the past to be redeemed, overcome, transformed and removed? What really is the past about? Let's look at the following notice.

Answering a divine job advert!

URGENT JOB VACANCY, ANYONE CAN APPLY, THERE ARE
NO AGE RESTRICTIONS

We are looking for exceptional people to undertake the helping of
others. For this role you will need experience that shows you know how
to come alongside those who are, for example ill, depressed, homeless
and abandoned. Of course there are many other needs than these. We
have listed only a few. There are many people in the world who are
suffering, and we want people to listen to and to understand others,
even if you may not always agree with what you hear from them.

The team we are hiring will form a worldwide organisation because
there is so much work to do – there is always need. Training is always
given – just take time alone with God to listen, and find others who can
support you, while you support them and others. Compassion needs a
place in the world, and you may need to fight for the needs of the
vulnerable in order to correct the prejudices and injustices. You will be
given blessings for this role. There are many ways in which this work
can be done so do not worry about how it unfolds, this will all be taken
care of. Each person who applies will be given this vocation in a way
that is suited to their own unique gifts and talents. We are always
recruiting! You can apply at anytime during your life, or even before it!

You will be looked after – but the only requirement is that if you
undertake this role you will have to live it in order to gain experience,
so that you are equipped to manage this job. This is the only way this
mission can be done; training has to be learnt on the job! This will be
costly and very painful at times, you may well wonder what you have
signed up for, but it is the only way. If you accept this role you will
learn wisdom! Everybody is called to this in some way; please let us
know if you want to apply. Heaven is taking your enquiries now!

This is a very broad, divine job advert. If you're experiencing
some of the difficulties listed in the advert, then it looks like

you've already applied (possibly without knowing) and are actually on the job! When we're on assignment we get hurt in order to learn empathy from this experience, so that it deepens our knowledge and equips us to develop those unique skills we will need to help those who are having similar troubles. Getting hurt though, doesn't mean it's OK, but often during a time of turbulence is when God plunges in to heal us by taking us back through our wounds in order to heal all that has destroyed us. When this happens we suddenly start to re-experience the past in a new redeemed way. It may have once seemed as though you were deserted by God but it was all part of your assignment. Now newness and healing come in through the wounds you may have suffered. Don't be afraid. This is when time for healing takes place, and new beneficial changes come into your life. You may also be in preparation for job promotion in your divine role.

Fulfilment of your mission – getting ready and then doing it

Now the assignment (the divine job advert) develops into the fulfilment of your mission. Once you were learning empathy from the wounds of the soul, now it's time to learn how you can heal with God's help. No longer the victim, (or however you may have perceived yourself), you become the person you were meant to be! Now is the time to fully be comfortable in the person you are, and find that is all you need. You have reached the place of empowerment. At the same time spiritual promotion comes in to give you joy and this can fill the void the past baggage once took up! All it needs is your permission to enter. Spiritual promotion doesn't mean life will be trouble free. It means you may now cope better with life because you have joy. As a consequence you may feel able to soar inside your spirit above all those difficulties rather than being sucked down by them. While this is happening are there any people you can teach how to recover? Allow God's redemptive light to come inside your soul to heal those wounds.

The key is asking for new confidence in yourself so you can keep out of the past. You may well need the memories of your past in order to help others through similar experiences. The difference is that now you will not be working out of your hurts to do this because you have overcome all that wounded you. Instead, you will be helping others to find their new way. Look forward to completing your mission in new and surprising ways, and remember that guidance comes in many forms.

Chapter Ten

Helping Others

Embracing a New Life – Living Your Onward Journey

Life is always about clear outs! Only, instead of looking around our homes and throwing out rubbish, and recycling, we're doing this inside us! Before we can go on and live more freely, we may need to take a closer look at our pasts. Are our habits still hindering us? Strong habits formed in our childhoods can remain. Have we really grown up? Are there any defence mechanisms in you which you needed as a child to protect yourself from any harsh goings on around you? Did you have one of those childhoods where you felt it was too much to handle and you had to roll yourself into a ball like a hedgehog to withdraw? You were well aware of the realities, but you had become like a sponge, soaked it up, didn't know what to do with it, and felt left to it. Many of us encounter happenings in our childhoods which influence our future, but don't serve us in adulthood. When we have difficulties handling stressful situations as an adult it is often because that child in us is panicking. The only way forward is to then unfurl as the hedgehog and release ourselves. We may have needed this protecting factor in our childhoods but do we need it as adults when we have work deadlines to meet, or we're busy raising families, or we just want to live in a more capable, less frantic mode of mind? Of course you may have had a great childhood, but there can still be patterns which are calling out to be released. Past habits are there to let out, not to keep! If you are still holding onto them – why are you keeping them? Can you bravely say goodbye to them, and embrace God's almighty power to fill you instead? We really don't want the past to dictate our present! (Even when we have a faith, it doesn't mean life is going to be easy!) It can be helpful to imagine that God's already helping us out of our unwanted habits because this stops us worrying about how we're going to get out of them!

Imagine arriving at a new destination, we have packed the luggage we want, we feel shiny and clean inside, and when we get there, we embrace the new view. The sun may be shining outside the window, and there may be a wonderful view of a beach with the waves sparkling in the sun. You may not like sitting in the sun, but it's there to warm you, and the view somehow reaches inside to relax you. So it is, when we move on, overcome, and start afresh. We may not actually go on holiday, but when we start to live anew our view of our own circumstances starts to get better. The same surroundings, but a new outlook!

What are you going to do with this new life? Even if you have overcome the past, habits may surface every now and again, but this time there's a difference, they won't stay, and you can live. Will and determination, and trusting in Jesus to get us there are invaluable sources of transformation.

Our onward journeys are heralded by a new season, new challenges, new perspectives, and sometimes new vocations! We have done some analysis of ourselves, we've learnt from it, and we can retrieve the wisdom in all our experiences to help others. We learn all the time, this journey will never stop, and it is as though we are perpetually on a train going from station to station. At each new station we learn something we weren't aware of at the last station. Somehow it all comes together to make us into the people we are. How are you going to use your wisdom? It's not fair to keep it to yourself!

How can we help our community and treat others well?

You may of course have always helped other people, when you can, but there may be some new ideas which you can now embrace:

Always be pleasant to people even if they annoy you, there are still ways of being nicely assertive! So many people never feel respected, and this can be why they are sometimes stroppy! Showing respect back to someone, even if you don't agree with them, can help them with self-belief!

Can you be a non-judgemental friend to those in need?

We are living in a culture where many people are working all hours for minimum pay and trying to pay their bills and mortgages, or rent. A lot of people are also getting into debt because of the amount of easy credit that cards make available. Consequently, people are living on adrenaline and in constant fear of homelessness, and any spare time is spent organising their lives so they can get through the next week in work. People in our society are breaking now, because of tension and pressure. Life is so hard. Do you have any skills you can use to train as a debt counsellor?

Can you help a homeless charity?

Is there any voluntary work you can commit to, even if it's an hour a month? So many of us don't have the time, but a small amount of time that we can agree to can make all the difference!

How many of us praise people in a shop, or any of the public services? Sometimes a letter or word of praise to their particular manager is a kindness that can leave people feeling appreciated and respected. This can be in direct contrast to the criticisms and hardness from the world.

Intentional vulnerability is a strength – but use it wisely and with discernment! Don't invite danger.

Sharing and being honest about the real life situations you've been in can help others get through similar life events too. For example, if a person approaches you with details of their ill health, career worries, or anything that's really getting them down, can you listen non-judgementally, and help them to feel safe? Do you know of any agencies or charities you could signpost them to? You are not responsible for how they may respond, so don't take sole responsibility for this person; you have instead given them a lifeline where they can contact specialists who may be able to help. Sometimes other people's problems are well out of our experience, so we can't take everything on. Be aware if you are feeling out of your depth, and keep yourself safe by realising this. All of us are experts in some way, but not in every single experience!

What are your neighbours like? Who are they?

Are there any neighbours you can help? Always have a boundary though, we all need the space in our own sanctuaries to come back to, in order to keep well and keep our energy, so always leave some energy for yourself!

Can you invite your neighbours to join you for a short time on Christmas Eve? Is it safe to ask your neighbours? If you do ask them, find out how many will be attending, and ask them to bring any mince pies or Christmas cake with them, you may all make new friends! Christmas can be so difficult for so many!

Can you invite anyone to join you for Christmas dinner? Can there be one extra place?

If the only parking space is in front of someone's drive, can you ring their bell and ask their permission, to park over it for a few minutes? If you just leave your car there, you can ruin the homeowners' day! What's going to happen to them if they can't get out of their drive? They may need to get to work, or attend an emergency!

Be mindful on the road, everyone's agenda is equally as important as the next person's, we all need to get somewhere in a time frame!

Make sure you always look after yourself even when you are busy and helping others!

It can be incredibly easy to lose yourself in helping other people, and sometimes it can become compulsive, an addiction! You might also experience a false sense of guilt if you believe you're not doing enough. Remember, we can only do so much, we are not machines and we need to take care of ourselves too. Look for a balance between the time to give, and the time to receive so that you make sure you always recharge what you have given away. Keep to a time boundary, especially when you are working to look after your own family! It's OK to have time off, and not feel guilty!

What have you learnt from those who you have helped? It is surprising how much in common we have with others! When a person confides in us, we may be able to identify with them, and in this way we too, receive. The danger here is letting their pain re-enter a similar past wound which you think you've overcome, but is still lurking within you. It can then become unbearable, and you are once again living with it. Try and empty yourself of your pain so that it leaves a space for you to listen to other people, but do not take on their problems. We cannot live another person's life for them. You may be a very empathic person, and find you are constantly worrying about them. But this can make you ill, while they may recover! Everybody has a different way of solving what they are going through, you can only advise, or listen. Too many of us carry a false guilt for many things for which we have no responsibility! Don't own everything in sight! Be aware of who owns what issue! People can put their own issues on us, so hand them back!

Don't compare yourself to anybody else. How someone else serves will be different from you, what another person can give will be different too! Look at what you can give, and not what others on your left and right are doing!

If you are unwell, please give yourself time to recover before you plunge back into life again! A friend used to tell me that sometimes illnesses come to remind us to rest!

It's OK to prioritise work commitments, and stick to them, and sometimes there will not be much time over to do anything else!

And finally live your life!

We will always encounter new growth and new problems, so don't be too fazed by this! New trials can seem scary when they spring upon us, so watch your responses to them! Our responses can determine if we can cope, or go under. Be realistic in what you feel, don't repress it, but always make a safe home within you to come back to. If you do not feel safe inside, imagine a wonderfully warm and friendly home inside you with God helping you to create this. Just imagining this can be a great tool for helping this to happen. This can help to transform any feelings of distress or alienation into a warm, homely feeling. It's safe to be you! Light is all around us, it might cloud over and become dark briefly, but like the sun, it will always come out again!

From the Author

Thank you for purchasing *Finding a Way Ahead*.

My sincere hope is that you derived as much help and advice from reading this book as I hoped for in creating it. If you have a few moments, please feel free to add your review of the book at your favorite online site for feedback (Amazon, GoodReads, etc.).

Also, if you would like more information about this or other works I have coming in the future please visit my website: *http://www.findingawayahead.com*

Sincerely, Angela Harper

Circle Books

CHRISTIAN FAITH

Circle Books explores a wide range of disciplines within the field of Christian faith and practice. It also draws on personal testimony and new ways of finding and expressing God's presence in the world today.

If you have enjoyed this book, why not tell other readers by posting a review on your preferred book site. Recent bestsellers from Circle Books are:

I Am With You (Paperback)
John Woolley
These words of divine encouragement were given to John Woolley in his work as a hospital chaplain, and have since inspired and uplifted tens of thousands, even changed their lives.
Paperback: 978-1-90381-699-8 ebook: 978-1-78099-485-7

God Calling
A. J. Russell
365 messages of encouragement channelled from Christ to two anonymous "Listeners".
Hardcover: 978-1-905047-42-0 ebook: 978-1-78099-486-4

The Long Road to Heaven
A Lent Course Based on the Film
Tim Heaton
This second Lent resource from the author of *The Naturalist and the Christ* explores Christian understandings of "salvation" in a five-part study based on the film *The Way*.
Paperback: 978-1-78279-274-1 ebook: 978-1-78279-273-4

Abide In My Love
More Divine Help for Today's Needs
John Woolley
The companion to I Am With You, Abide In My Love offers words of divine encouragement.
Paperback: 978-1-84694-276-1

From the Bottom of the Pond
The Forgotten Art of Experiencing God in the Depths of the Present Moment
Simon Small
From the Bottom of the Pond takes us into the depths of the present moment, to the only place where God can be found.
Paperback: 978-1-84694-066-8 ebook: 978-1-78099-207-5

God Is A Symbol Of Something True
Why You Don't Have to Choose Either a Literal Creator God or a Blind, Indifferent Universe
Jack Call
In this examination of modern spiritual dilemmas, Call offers the explanation that some of the most important elements of life are beyond our control: everything is fundamentally alright.
Paperback: 978-1-84694-244-0

The Scarlet Cord
Conversations With God's Chosen Women
Lindsay Hardin Freeman, Karen N. Canton
Voiceless wax figures no longer, twelve biblical women,
outspoken, independent, faithful, selfless risk-takers, come to
life in *The Scarlet Cord*.
Paperback: 978-1-84694-375-1

Will You Join in Our Crusade?
The Invitation of the Gospels Unlocked by the Inspiration of
Les Miserables
Steve Mann
Les Miserables' narrative is entwined with Bible study in this
book of 42 daily readings from the Gospels, perfect for Lent
or anytime.
Paperback: 978-1-78279-384-7 ebook: 978-1-78279-383-0

A Quiet Mind
Uniting Body, Mind and Emotions in Christian Spirituality
Eva McIntyre
A practical guide to finding peace in the present moment that
will change your life, heal your wounds and bring you a
quiet mind.
Paperback: 978-1-84694-507-6 ebook: 978-1-78099-005-7

Readers of ebooks can buy or view any of these bestsellers by clicking on the live link in the title. Most titles are published in paperback and as an ebook. Paperbacks are available in traditional bookshops. Both print and ebook formats are available online.

Find more titles and sign up to our readers' newsletter at http://www.johnhuntpublishing.com/christianity. Follow us on Facebook at https://www.facebook.com/ChristianAlternative.